DATE DUE

ENGINEERING DISABILITY

Public Policy and Compensatory Technology

HEALTH, SOCIETY, AND POLICY,
a series edited by Sheryl Ruzek and Irving Kenneth Zola

ENGINEERING DISABILITY

Public Policy and Compensatory Technology

Sandra J. Tanenbaum

TEMPLE UNIVERSITY PRESS
Philadelphia

Temple University Press, Philadelphia 19122

© 1986 by Temple University. All rights reserved
Published 1986

Printed in the United States of America

Library of Congress Cataloging-in-Publication Data

Tanenbaum, Sandra J.
  Engineering disability.

  (Health, society, and policy)
  Bibliography: p. 157
  Includes index.
  1. Prosthesis—Government policy—United States.
2. Orthopedic apparatus—Government policy—United
States.   3. Physically handicapped—Rehabilitation—
Government policy—United States.   I. Title.   II. Series.
RD130.T36   1986   362.4'0483   85-19684
ISBN 0-87722-403-X

Contents

Preface

The idea for this study predates my acquaintance with the Boston Elbow. I was led to this combination of subjects, rather, by the observation that social welfare policy can be made through the design and use of equipment-embodied technologies. Students of technology seemed to show little interest in social welfare and students of social welfare less interest in than mistrust of machines. Yet particularly in the field of disability, social and technological measures were being joined to achieve compensation. Surely something could be learned by studying them jointly.

I chose to do a case study in the face of myriad disability programs and rehabilitation technologies. I hoped to track disability benefits, hard and soft, through far-flung public welfare systems; the case study method would make this a coherent and manageable task. The Boston Elbow specifically was brought to my attention by people at M.I.T., where the device was originally designed. A sophisticated technological response to a basic human problem, the Boston Elbow promised to reveal the workings of disability policy in general.

Three M.I.T. professors—Harvey Sapolsky and Deborah Stone of the Political Science Department and Robert Mann of the Department of Mechanical Engineering—agreed to guide my work. I would like to thank them as well as Richard Sclove and Mark Segal, then at M.I.T., and several anonymous reviewers for the Office of Technology Assessment (which published an abbreviated case study

of the Boston Elbow) for comments on earlier drafts of this book. I
of course remain responsible for any errors of fact or judgment.

The Kaiser Family Foundation lent this research financial support. Janet Francendese, Jennifer French, and Doris Braendel of Temple University Press shepherded the manuscript (and the author) through publication. I would also like to thank Adrienne Mendell and Lee Dante, who inspired my first technology assessment, and Will Batstone, friend and comfort, for always understanding about the book.

ENGINEERING DISABILITY

Public Policy and Compensatory Technology

I

Introduction

Public Policy and Compensatory Technology

This is a story about the ways in which government responds to functional loss among the citizenry. Disability is a public problem (Gusfield, 1981) as well as a deeply personal one; functional loss necessitates public expenditures for health care and income maintenance and has created a disability rights movement. But government's response may take many forms—individual and collective, physical and social. Increasingly, public policy may also diffuse rehabilitation technologies—that is, devices that compensate for the user's physical disability.

The story that follows is about the conditions under which government diffuses these technologies. It is about which disabled people receive compensatory devices and their alternatives: income maintenance, physical therapy, protection of civil rights, and others. It is about the origins of disability policy and the implications of multiple social welfare systems for the diffusion of rehabilitation technologies.

This story is a new story. It is about social policy, but focuses on hardware. It is about the diffusion of technology, but dwells on the social meanings of devices. Its premise is that disability is a loss—of function and correspondingly of mobility, employability, and the like—and it maintains that disability policy, in distributing compensation for these losses, redistributes loss itself. The design of disability benefits is a political process. Government diffuses rehabilitation

technologies less by building better mousetraps and more by de-
ciding whose mice are entitled to be trapped.

The story that follows is a research essay (Gusfield, 1981) that
views contextually the public diffusion of compensatory technologies. It brings to bear case material about the Boston Elbow—a sophisticated arm prosthesis worn by about one hundred people with
upper-extremity amputations—but does not rely on these data to
make its point. Rather, the case of the Boston Elbow is illustrative,
chosen for practical and substantive reasons. First, the designers and
manufacturer of the device were willing to discuss it at length. Second, the case represents the application of current engineering science and conventional prosthetics practice to an old and unambiguous problem, the loss of a limb. Finally, the Elbow is no longer a
prototype; it is an element of the existing health care system, worn
by people who acquired it with expectations of functionality. As will
be noted in Chapter 6, the particulars of developing and diffusing
the Boston Elbow are not generalizable even to a sophisticated knee
prosthesis. Still, discussion of the elbow is revealing. It provides raw
material for competing conceptual frameworks and will be drawn
over the contextual framework proposed below.

The research for this study was done with primary and secondary written sources and through unstructured interviews with approximately eighty participants in and observers of the diffusion of
rehabilitation technologies. Individuals interviewed included rehabilitation engineers, physicians, prosthetists, physical/occupational
therapists, insurers, and people with disabilities. Interviews were
also conducted with current and former government officials at the
state and federal levels and in virtually every disability program related to use of a prosthesis: workers' compensation, Social Security
Disability Insurance, Supplemental Security Income, Medicare,
Medicaid, independent living, Vocational Rehabilitation, and veterans disability benefits. Disability activists, including officials and
members of voluntary organizations (for example, the American Coalition of Citizens with Disabilities) were important sources of information. Scholars of disability and members of disability-related professional organizations—for example, the American Orthotics and
Prosthetics Association—also contributed to the study, as did medi-

cal directors for two large for-profit insurance firms. Finally, a number of HMO officials were surveyed by telephone. Interviews were generally conducted with the understanding that sources would not be identified by name. They are therefore frequently described below with reference to profession, program, organization, or disability, whichever pertains.

Individuals chosen for interviews were those who seemed most likely to contribute to the breadth, depth, and accuracy of the information gathered. One good source would frequently recommend another, and interviews were sought with individuals who had made relevant contributions to the diffusion and rehabilitation literatures. People who were prominent in their fields of expertise or who played an important role in diffusing the Boston Elbow were contacted first. Most of the interviews for this study were done as dissertation research, and sources were so advised.

Disability policy is made and carried out at the state as well as federal level. Workers' compensation, Medicaid, and the Vocational Rehabilitation Program are, in fact, primarily state responsibilities. In this essay, Massachusetts will serve as a proxy for all the states; disability policy there will provide the particulars for analysis. This is not to claim that Massachusetts is representative of the other states. It is not. But close study of more than one state is impractical here, and generalizations across states reveal less than does scrutiny of one set of programs. Massachusetts was the obvious choice for a study of the Boston Elbow. And although states vary significantly in their responses to disability, they, like Massachusetts, all respond differently to different classes of disabled people.

A final introductory remark concerns the word "technology." For the purpose of this study, "technology" denotes hardware, what Langdon Winner (1977, p. 11) calls "apparatus," or what is sometimes referred to as "equipment-embodied" technology. Technology might be interpreted more broadly to mean any process or system that achieves a desired end, but such a definition would overstate the intention of this study. It is precisely the diffusion of rehabilitation *hardware* that is of interest here. Social policy is widely appreciated as a purveyor of "soft" technologies such as education and psychotherapy. Policy is itself a soft technology. But this social policy analysis is designed to emphasize something else—the otherwise over-looked machines with which social policy is sometimes carried out.

The Diffusion of Compensatory Technologies: A Framework

Government may respond to functional loss by diffusing compensatory technologies. Chapters 2, 3, and 4 will discuss how this response affects disabled veterans, workers, and citizens. At a more general level, this study views the diffusion of compensatory technology in a framework that departs significantly from models articulated elsewhere. The framework presented here allows for consideration of two *contextual* aspects of diffusion. First, what are the alternatives to the technology in question? How else might the user respond to functional loss? Second, what is the relationship between the user and the diffuser? How is the one defined for and identified by the other? Non-technological strategies for dealing with functional loss always exist; these create the context for diffusing compensatory technologies. Furthermore, when government diffuses devices, it does so in accordance with distributive principles based on the relationship between the user and the state.

Rehabilitation technologies mitigate *functional loss,* and an understanding of this compensatory aspect suggests the framework offered here. First, functional loss is basic and serious. By definition, it is an inability to carry out major activities of daily living, and it resembles physical and mental illness in this regard. Technologies for people with disabilities, then, are more like biomedical technologies than, say, consumer goods. They bring with them a retinue of experts—physicians, prosthetists, and others. In some sense, the professional is the consumer to whom compensatory technologies, like other medical technologies, diffuse; physicians prescribe prostheses, and prosthetists order and modify limb components, for example. Unlike illness, functional loss is, secondly, embedded and idiosyncratic. It is by definition the frustration of an individual's efforts to get along in his or her own environment. Disabled individuals may not understand the physiological basis of what they experience, but they know best its functional implications. There are many ways to meet a functional need, and humans design compensatory strategies by bringing to bear myriad details of residual functioning and of the environments with which they must contend. Thus the framework presented here is built around the potential user of the Boston Elbow. It applies as well to all people who suffer functional loss because it depicts the ways in which they may choose among and combine competing compensatory measures. The framework will be explicated at length below. It is best understood, however, with reference to the prevailing models of technological innovation.

The "Lifecycle" Model

The most prevalent model of technological innovation can be called the "lifecycle" model and is depicted in Figure 1. It posits a series of stages through which all new devices pass. Diffusion is the final or near-final stage, when the technology in question is actually put to use. The lifecycle model is organized around the device, which, according to this view, begins as an idea and matures into a product. One presentation of the model treats biomedical technology specifically and identifies four stages in the innovation process: idea generation; idea communication; the development of clinical applications; and the appearance of resultant products in the market (Moskowitz et al., 1981). A more disaggregated biomedical example begins with basic research and progresses through applied research, development, use, clinical trials, and adoption, to acceptance (Banta and Behney, 1981). Figure 1 was itself redrawn from one study of rehabilitation technology (Muthard, 1980; cited OTA, 1982, p. 97) and has been used in at least one other, conducted by the U.S. Congress.

The metaphor that underlies this model—the lifecycle of an inanimate product—pervades general and biomedical diffusion research. The lifecycle is both descriptive and normative, casting innovation as natural and developmental and suggesting that intervention take the form of support for or facilitation of the process. As assistant secretary for health, Julius Richmond called on the De-

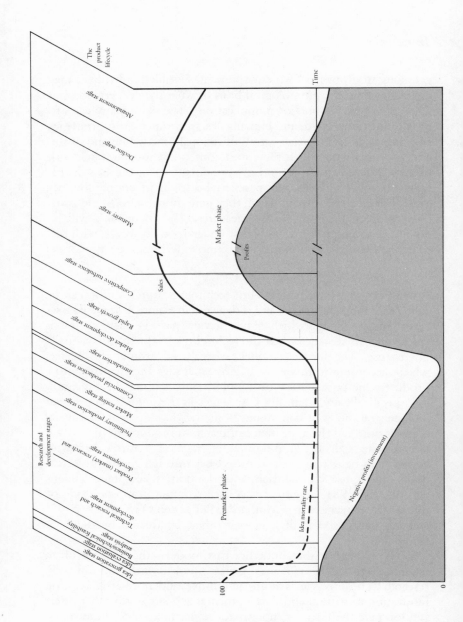

THE INNOVATION PROCESS
Figure 1

Source: Redrawn from Muthard, 1980; cited OTA, 1982, p. 97.

partment of Health, Education, and Welfare to devise ways to "link" the stages of the technological lifecycle (cited in Moskowitz et al., 1981, p. 2). Harvey Brooks elaborates the metaphor when he relates technological to biological evolution. He compares what he calls the "inherent logic of technological development" with the genetic inheritance of an organism. Natural selection of a technology occurs through various social mechanisms, including the market; competing technologies take on the role of other species (Brooks, 1980, p. 68).

The "Communications" Model
A second model of technological innovation can be called the "communications" model. It focuses on exchanges of information among individuals involved in the innovation process and is useful in identifying the key actors and personal characteristics that seem to generate communication about new technologies. The classic application of the communications model to biomedical technology is the 1966 study by J. S. Coleman, E. Katz, and H. Menzel of drug diffusion in the medical community. They found that the decision to adopt a new drug therapy was frequently the result of verbal communication from "innovative" physicians to their more cautious colleagues and that innovators tended to have higher incomes, larger practices, and a more cosmopolitan orientation. In the general innovation literature, Thomas J. Allen writes about the importance of organizational "gatekeepers"—those individuals who channel the flow of new information into a firm (Allen, 1977). He has found that employees' job mobility, university acquaintances, and attendance at professional meetings have an effect on how much information comes to the firm from outside sources (Allen, 1981). Students of biomedical innovation describe comparable communication among researchers and between researchers and practitioners (Moskowitz et al., 1981).

The Contextual Framework
The framework offered below departs from the lifecycle and communications models. Unlike the lifecycle model, it does not focus on devices. Technologies for people with disabilities are the sub-

ject of this study, but they are considered throughout as only one of the disabled person's many options. Similarly, the Boston Elbow is shown to have developed over a period of years, but its lifecycle is given less attention than its use at any one time.

Like the communications model, the framework for this study is built around humans in the diffusion process. Communications research, however, looks primarily at professionals rather than users, and one can argue that as healers, physicians are the real users of biomedical technology. In the case of compensatory technologies, this argument is unconvincing; to be useful, rehabilitative devices must be woven into the disabled person's day-to-day life. A more serious difference between the communications model and the framework presented here is that the latter can be used to depict sets of options available to classes of persons with amputations. The communications model assumes that diffusion occurs when individuals exchange information: gatekeepers link engineers; physicians depend upon informed colleagues. In this study it is argued that, while individual disabled people and rehabilitation professionals may communicate about developments in compensatory technology, there are contextual reasons why some devices reach or do not reach some people. As will be made clear below, public policy sorts people into classes, and different classes face different sets of compensatory options. These sets are not arbitrary. They reflect the purposes and histories of the policies that create them.

Consider Figure 2, an alternative framework for understanding technological diffusion. The point of origin is an individual's functional loss, and an array of possible compensatory measures follows. Figure 2 was fashioned specifically for the case of the Boston Elbow. It is the set of choices facing a person with an above-elbow amputation. But many of these measures also apply to people with other disabilities, and even if they do not, similar choices do. Figure 2 is meant to convey the following: that having lost an arm above the elbow, an individual may or may not wear a Boston Elbow. There are other possible responses to the loss, and they are most clearly viewed as the non-exclusive branches of a decision tree.

First, a compensatory measure may target the disabled person or his or her environment. Is the result to be a changed human, or

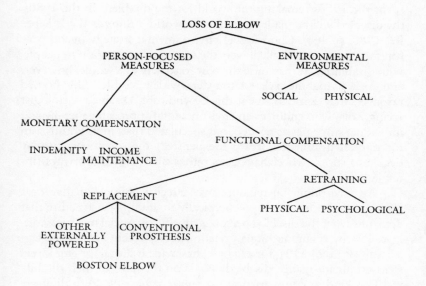

——— Possible responses

A FRAMEWORK FOR VIEWING RESPONSES TO LOSS OF AN ARM
Figure 2

are the surroundings to be altered? This choice arises repeatedly in disability policy-making. One rehabilitation expert, referring to recent advances in technologies like the Boston Elbow, stated: "We spent the 1970s remaking the world for the disabled. In the 1980s the disabled will be made ready for the world" (*Business Week*, Sept. 22, 1980, p. 46c). Choosing an environmental strategy over a person-focused one generally lowers the cost of compensation to people with disabilities. It may raise the cost to society as a whole, however, and makes disability-related transfers widely visible. Able-bodied taxpayers may come to resent this expenditure. Disabled sociologist Irving Zola, who endorses an environmental approach generally and individual strategies as needed, has speculated that, in its enthusiasm for non-environmental (read: inexpensive) measures, society may decide to shrink wheelchair users rather than widen doorways (interview).

An environmental measure may effect a physical change or a social one. The former is prototypically the ramp—a structure that demands what the disabled person is capable of. Social measures mitigate loss by changing human relationships. Recent civil rights legislation (P.L. 93-112), for example, has made it illegal for employers to discriminate against disabled people on the basis of their disability. This kind of compensation may make it possible for a disabled person to hold a desirable job and so to recover some of what was lost through illness or injury.

A person-focused approach may be monetary or functional in nature, and two monetary strategies supplement the disabled person's assets. An indemnity is a previously established sum considered fair compensation for anatomical loss. Workers' compensation programs generally include such a benefit; loss of an arm above the elbow, for example, brings a person a fixed sum. A second kind of monetary strategy is income maintenance. This is an ongoing program of cash transfers, usually scaled to need, and based on the assumption that amputation has a negative effect on labor force participation.

A functional strategy is one that actually restores the capacity to function in daily life. It has two variations, retraining and replacement. Retraining is predicated on the permanent loss of some body part and prepares the individual for life without it. This is a common choice among persons with unilateral upper-extremity amputations, for example. Even prosthetists admit that it is possible, especially with training, to do most of what is essential with only one arm (interviews). Retraining may be psychological as well as physical; the rehabilitation process usually entails a coming to terms with loss. In fact, a blind speaker at a recent workshop on rehabilitation technology told his audience that their approach to disability was counterproductive and certain to fail. He argued that replacement serves only to impede adaptation, which he defines as the disabled individual's developing a set of compensatory beliefs and behaviors (Madjid, 1982).

Figure 2's final set of compensatory measures is alternative replacement technologies—in this case, the Boston Elbow, other externally powered elbows, and the body-powered cable elbow. These devices are perhaps the most obvious response to disability, and they are in the minds of many the most promising.

The contextual framework for understanding diffusion of the Boston Elbow and other rehabilitation technologies is an array of measures for mitigating disability. How, then, does a potential user choose among them? Seemingly, he or she does so on two grounds. The first is the category into which, for public policy purposes, the user falls—that is, the set of disability-related benefits he or she receives as veteran, worker, or citizen. These will be charted in Chapters 2, 3, and 4 below.

The second ground is what might be called meaning—how the person who has suffered an amputation understands the loss and the possibilities for compensation. In his book *Loss and Change* Peter Marris examines responses to loss of various kinds (Marris, 1974). He observes that no matter what sort of loss people suffer, they always meet it with grief, and that this is true even when the loss is a result of desired change. People seem to long for predictability, for the meaning inherent in continuity. Marris calls this tendency people's "conservative impulse" (p. 7). Although it is their nature to grow and change, they adapt to change by applying an already held construction of reality. Change is necessary but painful. It inspires ambivalence in the person who is changing, who wants to give up the past but also to hold on to it.

According to Marris, grief is the process whereby this ambivalence is resolved. It is "a working out of conflicting impulses" (p. 31) to hold on and to let go. Grief succeeds when it extracts a meaning from the past and finds that meaning again in the future. In a passage that unwittingly connects disability with other losses, Marris says, "The fundamental crisis of bereavement arises, not from the loss of others, but the loss of self" (p. 36). It is possible to come to terms with change by recapturing the lost aspect of self, the meaning for self of what has passed. In this context, innovation is essentially a buffer against frustration of purpose, and while Marris does not discuss equipment-embodied technological innovation, his argument holds. The innovator does something new to sustain an old identity. Prosthesis makers allow users to confirm their identities by restoring a part of them that has been lost.

Identity emerges repeatedly as a factor in choosing among compensatory strategies. Max Cleland, former head of the Veterans Administration, lost both legs and an arm in Vietnam. He relates the counsel of a friend who watched him climbing stairs on two artificial legs: "'Max,' she asked in concern, 'why are you wearing those things?' Then she put her hand on my arm. 'We love you the way you are.' . . . I needed to come to terms with the fact that *I* had to love me the way I was too" (Cleland, 1980, p. 144). Cleland was relieved when his physician ordered him off his leg prostheses: "Somehow my machismo had been involved in walking on those legs" (p. 142). Another person with an amputation, who is also a physical therapist, has surmised that, for some, not wearing a prosthesis is a political act, a "flag" for communicating that people with disabilities are also people. She herself does not wear a prosthesis, both because she is uncomfortable in the one she can afford and because she wants to show other people that she is functional and working despite her disability (interview).

No one can make disabled people able-bodied. No prosthesis can restore a lost arm, and some of its features must be chosen over others. Marris' understanding of grief is useful here. It suggests that coming to terms with amputation, for example, involves extracting from two-armedness the most important aspects, the ones that most directly defined the individual before his or her loss. Because technologies and other compensatory measures replace some functions, their compensatory power depends on the sensitivity and wisdom with which a particular measure is matched to a particular user. How does one match person and machine?

At a 1982 meeting of rehabilitation professionals and consumers of compensatory devices, one engineer urged his colleagues to "let the light of technology shine" on disability (McLaurin, 1982). A less positive exhortation came from prosthetics experts who claimed in 1973 that "no serious attempt has been made to apply a rational approach to the matching of man and machine" (Murdoch and Hughes, 1973, p. 70). Of what would such a rational response consist? What exactly *is* the light of technology? Rehabilitation technologies spring from a desire to mitigate functional loss. It is not obvious, however, just how to mitigate armlessness or other disabilities. In 1977, the rehabilitation technology field seemed unable even to define its task (Ayers, 1977).

Why not simply replicate the human arm? D. S. McKenzie speaks for the more reflective engineer when he asserts:

> The natural arm is in many ways a perfect instrument. It embodies multiple degrees of freedom all capable of integrated function. . . .
> It is manifestly unrealistic to think one could write down all the criteria and performance specifications of the normal arm and hope even to begin to be able to reproduce them in a man-made device (McKenzie, 1969, p. 363).

Moreover, replacing the natural limb necessarily alters the body system radically and precludes, by definition, real replication of the natural arm (Kenedi, 1969). Regardless of existing technological capabilities, "it is important to keep in mind that a prosthesis is a very poor substitute for a normal limb" (O'Sullivan et al., 1981, p. 365).

The human body cannot be replicated, but humans can fashion some kind of compensatory device. The device will embody only a subset of the functions and meanings of what was lost, and these choices are complex. Judgments will be wrought again and again. Some needs will emerge only when others are attended to (Schon, 1967). What should obtain in an arm prosthesis, for example, may become evident only after a provisional device has been fitted. Engineers and prosthetists disagree among themselves about which should receive the highest priority. Dudley Childress chooses positioning the hook or hand in space and in relation to the other arm as the objective toward which artificial arm design should proceed (Childress, 1973). Others have stressed sensation in the upper extremity, particularly in the hook or hand, which they contend cannot function in any satisfactory way without sensory feedback. The variety of possible approaches to the design of an arm is startling. At the most basic level, there is the gross dichotomy between starting from first principles and improving existing prostheses (Fulford and Hall, 1968). A more disaggregated list reads: simulation of normal arm movement (for example, force and trajectory), faithful re-creation of command outputs and sensory inputs, design for specific tasks (for example, feeding), and working either from hand to shoulder function or vice versa (McKenzie, 1969). Functional and cosmetic goals may conflict. And evaluating the fruits of the design process means raising these and other issues all over again. Should evaluation focus on engineering values, functional capacities, mental workload, consumer satisfaction? Even the most comprehensive study entails choosing how to weight the several variables. Stephen Jacobsen notes that because explicit evaluation of prosthetic limbs means considering so many factors, design decisions are often made intuitively (Jacobsen et al., 1982). Similarly, McKenzie anticipates that in the face of the natural arm's broad functionality, "each worker will seize on a particular feature he wishes to sustain . . . and a multiplicity of attempted 'solutions' is inevitable" (McKenzie, 1969, p. 363).

How do some solutions come to be chosen over others? By what method are specific functions identified for replacement? M.I.T. engineer Neville Hogan holds that the design process begins with the recognition that no prosthesis can replace what has been lost. A series of trade-offs follows, defined by the current boundaries of neurophysiology and engineering science (interview). Jacobsen, who has created a second-generation Elbow called the "Utah Arm," admits to a "general design philosophy" among the engineers with whom he works; it derives from the group and is made clear to all participants in the Utah Arm project (Jacobsen et al., 1982, p. 251).

Other students of technology are more explicit about the normative aspect of design. Donald W. Shriver, Jr., for example, asserts:

"Bertrand Russell had hold of some truth when he said, 'Whatever else is mechanical, values are not.' But the remark was libelous of machinery. A flipped over version of Russell's remark would be the analysis that philosophers probably need more to hear: *Whatever else is valueless, machines are not*" (Shriver, 1973, p. 8). Machines are not valueless, because their design is a series of human choices. Designers value some purposes and qualities over others, and technologies attest to these biases in their shapes, sizes, materials, and so on. Langdon Winner pursues the point further, specifying two ways in which technology not only represents values but "legislates" them (Winner, 1980, p. 317). Winner argues that technology is legislation first when it necessitates laws about the risk, cost, and distribution of machines. This is a common occurrence. Toxic waste and nuclear power legislation assign risk to people living near dumps and reactors. Medicare coverage of kidney dialysis has meant the assumption of high costs by the Social Security system. Airline deregulation seriously limited the availability of air travel to people along lightly traveled routes.

Winner's second point is that technology not only demands legislation; it actually does what legislation does—that is, it structures relationships among people. Winner cites Frederick Engels' example of the dictatorial relationship between captain and crew on large sailing vessels. Another example is the extent to which kneeling busses and wheelchair-accessible buildings make people with disabilities more visible to able-bodied people. Again, advances in neonatal medical technology shape the relationships among abortion-seeking women, their physicians, and the state. Technology's normative aspect originates in but is not limited to the design phase. A device may take on meanings as it is used by different individuals in different contexts (Shriver, 1973). Did the electronics engineers who designed "ghetto blasters" have in mind the creation of an urban flashpoint? Robert Pirsig describes at length the way in which users of technology may exercise their values:

> Technology presumes there's just one right way to do things and there never is. And when you presume there's just one right way to do things, of *course* the instructions begin and end exclusively with

the [object to be assembled]. But if you have to choose among an infinite number of ways to put it together then the relation of the machine to you, and the relation of the machine and you to the rest of the world, has to be considered, because the selection from among many choices, the *art* of the work is just as dependent upon your own mind and spirit as it is upon the material of the machine (Pirsig, 1974, pp. 147–148).

Designing an above-elbow prosthesis means taking a position whose coordinates lie along several dimensions. Cost is of course one, with private and even public sector engineers focused on the tally: how much of any other factor is worth its cost? Finite resources may also force a choice between providing more expensive technologies to fewer people and providing less expensive devices to many more, especially in cases where the marginal cost of increased functioning rises steeply. Absolute, marginal, unit, program, covered, uncovered, and opportunity costs may all figure in the design of rehabilitation technologies.

A second dimension is the value given to "advanced" machines—the continuum between low and high technology. Sophisticated devices may gratify physicians and engineers more than they benefit consumers, who, according to one physiatrist, have "limited gadget tolerance" (interview). Yet some disabled consumers seem to prefer high to low technology. They desire extension of their physical functioning and, like many able-bodied Americans, favor souped-up machines over ordinary ones. Rehabilitation engineers interviewed for this study have been struck by an apparent acceptance of the blatantly technological. Consumers seem eager to adopt complex technologies such as cameras and home computers. Similarly, some quadraplegic people favor manipulators over limb braces. Although manipulators are more robotic in their appearance, they can be programmed to execute a series of movements and are thus functionally more powerful than limb braces are. Still, high technologies are likely to be costly and difficult to maintain.

A variation on the high/low technology dimension is what Robert Mann calls "access"/"innateness"—access being how safe and convenient a prosthesis is and innateness the degree to which control of the machine replicates control of the natural arm. Access and innateness may trade off. A device that is easy to understand and maintain will probably not achieve the sophistication that characterizes the relationship of a human to his extremities. In their attempt to replicate control of the natural arm, participants in the Boston Elbow project fashioned a highly complex machine (Mann, 1973).

One of the most widely held consumer values is cosmesis—attractiveness—which, to the extent that it trades off against functionality, constitutes a third dimension. Cosmesis is dynamic as well as static; a desirable prosthesis looks and acts like a limb. But what is most natural-looking may not be obvious. A cosmetic glove on an artificial hand, for example, may give the hand a robotic look, especially compared with steel hooks used dextrously (McKenzie, 1969). The ideal prosthesis becomes a part of the user's body. He or she incorporates it into an expanded body image and ceases to view it as a foreign object (Canestrari and Ricci Bitti, 1978).

A fourth dimension is the ease/growth trade-off. A compensatory technology should serve the user, but should it not also stretch his functional capabilities? What is the proper division of labor between person and machine? Physiatrist Paul Corcoran finds that too little attention is paid to a patient's residual abilities. Much could be learned, he argues, by paying more attention to the ways in which people with disabilities learn to compensate (Corcoran, 1978; also Kornbluh, 1981). Transparency is also important in this context: no matter how many functions a machine performs, as long as the disabled user controls the device and remains visible "through" it, it is an extension of him or her and not vice versa (interview with rehabilitation engineer). Corcoran objects to expressions like "confined to crutches" or "wheelchair bound." For someone with the appropriate impairment, he points out, these technologies can be a liberation and should be appreciated as such (Corcoran, 1978). Similarly, some disability activists argue that use of a compensatory technology need not constitute a state of dependency. Rather, independence is access to tools and helpers. Zola, for example, says: "It is not the quantity of tasks we can perform without assistance but the quality of life we can live with help" (Zola, 1980, p. 4). Use of a compensatory technology may be discretionary; the user may be able to function without a device, but choose to use it in order to conserve energy. Zola has made this choice, for example, by using a wheelchair when he could walk with braces, thereby arriving fresh at his destination. He considers this social and psychological independence at the cost of someone else's idea of physical independence (Zola, 1980).

It is argued above that functional loss is both basic and serious, embedded and idiosyncratic. Conceiving compensatory strategies, then, requires user involvement as well as professional attention, and disabled consumers are eager to join engineers, physicians, and prosthetists in creating rehabilitative devices. The ideal role for consumers of compensatory technology is topical (for example, OTA, 1982; Stern and Redden, eds., 1982). It is an appropriate theme with which to close this presentation of a user-created diffusion framework.

Potential consumers of rehabilitation technologies are frequently endorsed as participants in the design process. Neither the engineer nor the policy analyst can fully determine the usefulness of a particular machine; cost benefit analysis in particular is suspect as a guide in matters of rehabilitation (Noble, 1976; OTA, 1982). An official of the American Association for the Advancement of Science's project on science and disability, argued that the relative lack of participation by people with disabilities in the design of compensatory technology is the major reason these devices do not diffuse. Drawing on his experience with disabled consumers, he concluded that existing technologies simply do not meet the needs of their market (interview). Increased participation may be achieved in several ways. Disabled people can work to broaden the views of able-bodied engineers, act as subjects in or on advisory panels for research and development, or provide information to other potential consumers (Kornbluh, 1981). One disability activist described the ideal participant as someone with a relevant disability who uses or would use the technology in question, is mature and knowledgeable, and is in contact with the larger disabled community (Pfrommer, 1982). As Zola points out, one sort of consumer participation is already underway—that is, people with disabilities regularly modify the devices they use. Zola concludes that, although such efforts may appear to be attempts to improve the devices, they are rather efforts to personalize them (Zola, 1980).

Consumer participation is not universally endorsed. Some engineers argue that disabled people without engineering training cannot appreciate the exigencies of design, that such participants are simply not prepared to discuss the technical aspects of the machine (interview with rehabilitation engineer/government official). One rehabilitation engineer fears progress will actually be slowed by consumers who do not understand the need for basic research (interview). Furthermore, political and philosophical differences among people with disabilities can complicate participation. Which point of view is to be attended to (Brown and Redden, 1979)? One able-bodied rehabilitation engineer resolved the matter for himself; he traveled the Boston public transportation system in a wheelchair.

The design of a prosthesis, then, requires judgments along the dimensions of cost, high/low technology, cosmesis/functionality, ease/growth, and user participation. It should be noted, finally, that decisions about these many factors may be made at various levels of aggregation. To whom is the cost of a technology assigned: any one user, all users, government, other third-party payers? Does the value purchased accrue at the same level as the cost, or is there an inter-level transfer? Similarly, does consumer participation mean involvement of the actual user, a disabled individual representing users, a non-user representing users? How responsive to the varying needs of individual users should the design of any compensatory technology be?

The User

Who is the potential user of the Boston Elbow and how do his or her characteristics affect its diffusion? The number of persons with upper-extremity amputations in the United States is set at about 100,000 (Mann, 1981, p. 4). It has been estimated from unusually detailed data collected in 1967 (Davies et al., 1970, p. 21) that 43 percent of the number of persons with upper-extremity amputations (some of these being bilateral) fitted with a prosthesis have above-elbow amputations, and the 1977 National Health Interview Survey (NCHS, 1980, cited Theta Technology Corp., 1981, p. 11) found the number of persons with above-elbow amputations to be about 53,000, or 58 percent of all upper-extremity amputations. The 15 percent discrepancy may reflect the fact that many persons with above-elbow amputations are never fitted with prostheses. More plentiful and recent data are about limb amputation generally. The National Health Interview Survey found in 1977 that approximately 358,000 Americans had lost at least one major extremity. But lower-extremity amputation is far more common—perhaps as much as ten times more common—than upper-extremity amputation. (The 258,000 figure, only 2.5 times 100,000, probably refers to persons with leg as opposed to foot amputations, and many of these individuals are likely to have a bilateral loss.) Because above-elbow amputations account for so small a percentage of the total, statistical pictures drawn of persons with amputations as a group do not provide much information about the potential wearer of the Boston Elbow. Most importantly, upper-extremity amputation usually results from trauma and lower-extremity amputation from vascular disease (Kerstein, 1980). The person with an above-elbow amputation is therefore likely to be younger than his or her lower-extremity counterpart, to be in better general health, and more often to have been employed preceding the loss. This would seem to bode well for public diffusion of the Boston Elbow. A young, healthy person who has been employed is likely to seem a worthy recipient of a sophisticated prosthesis.

"Amputation" denotes loss of an extremity from any cause. Using this definition, it was estimated in a study of 8,700 persons fitted with prostheses that 9 percent of above-elbow amputations are congenital. (This number is presumably higher in those countries where the drug thalidomide was widely used.) Eight percent result from tumors, 6 percent from disease, and 77 percent from trauma (Davies et al., 1970, p. 22). Of 723 trauma-related upper-extremity amputations identified by cause, industrial, farm, and automobile accidents accounted for almost all amputations in women and 68 percent of the amputations in men. War was cited in another 7 percent of the upper-extremity amputations in men, who are far more likely than women to lose an arm above the elbow for any reason (Davies et al., 1970, p. 30).

Amputation as a surgical procedure is relatively straightforward. It is usually undertaken to revise a congenital or acquired deformity or as a last resort in treating trauma or diseases like cancer, diabetes, and vascular disease. One-year mortality rates for persons with amputations have plummeted since 1930, when persons with lower-extremity amputations had an equal chance of dying as living in the first year following the loss (Corcoran, 1981). Still, amputation surgery is criticized publicly by patients and their advocates (Kerstein, 1980; Whipple, 1980). They make two charges: that amputations are relegated to the least experienced surgical residents because this surgery is considered elementary and inconsequential to successful rehabilitation; and that even the most experienced and conscientious surgeon is likely to favor saving as much of a limb as possible, often leaving a stump that is difficult, or even impossible, to fit with a prosthesis (Murdoch, 1969; interview with rehabilitation engineer). Recent reforms in surgical practice acknowledge the role of prosthetics in surgical care. Physicians are beginning to perform amputations that leave fewer scars and maximize residual muscle power. Some surgeons have begun to invite prosthetists into the operating room (Murdoch and Hughes, 1973).

What is a person's status after amputation? What are the parameters of his or her loss, and does it constitute a disability? The answers to these questions depend in part on the way in which disability is defined, and alternative meanings proliferate. For the purposes of this chapter, "disability" will denote, following Saad Z. Nagi, "a pattern of behavior that evolves when impairments impose limitations upon the individual's capacities and levels of functioning" (Nagi, 1969, p. 12). Impairment is an "anatomical, physiological, intellectual, or emotional abnormality or loss" and results in disability when the impaired individual is constrained by his or her condition. Many impairments, including amputation, are assumed to impose limitations on functioning. Whether these disabilities become handicaps, however, depends on the environment in which the disabled individual functions. The Office of Technology Assessment (OTA), in its *Technology and Handicapped People*, defines a handicap as a "socially, environmentally and personally specified limitation" (OTA, 1982). Even an able-bodied person can be handicapped by an obstacle-ridden environment. Amputation, then, is always an impairment; it is a disability for most people, and it is conceivably a handicap, depending on the person's individual circumstances.

Amputation as a disabling condition has serious implications for other aspects of a person's life. Specifying these losses, however, should proceed with the caveat that disability data are replete with weaknesses. Serious students of disability complain that the field has no quantitative theory meeting validity and reliability standards, and that except for studies focused on intervention at the individual level, disability research has received too few funds (Howards et al., 1980). One researcher observed that, although service providers consider current assessment capabilities satisfactory, academics generally fault either particular methodologies or the conceptualization of disability as a social problem (interview). It is frequently recommended that measures of disability be function- rather than symptom-based and standardized to the greatest extent possible (Howards et al., 1980; Dudek and Brewer, 1978).

Perhaps the most significant weakness in disability data is that whether or not an individual is "disabled" seems itself to depend on factors other than limitations on functioning. In a 1980 study, Irving Howards, Henry P. Brehm, and Saad Z. Nagi researched the relationship between the disability rate in a particular geographical area and selected variables reflecting the socioeconomic status of its inhabitants. The investigation found that socioeconomic factors explained 82 percent of the variance in disability (self-reported to a census-taker) across areas, with the percentage of households making less than $4,000 accounting for over 51 percent. This measure of poverty explained more than any other single variable. When Howards et al. disaggregated the data into severely and partially disabled persons, they found that socioeconomic variables explained as much as 88 percent and poverty alone 45 percent of the variance in severe disability; persons who defined themselves as partially disabled emerged as a swing group between disabled and non-disabled persons depending on the local economy. It seems that in any geographic area, there are some number of self-defined disabled people who in times of prosperity make no claims on the disability system but respond to economic adversity by taking up a disabled status (Howards et al., 1980). Levitan and Taggart observe a similar phenomenon: in time of high unemployment, less severely disabled people are likely to lose positions in the competitive labor market and avail themselves of jobs targeted specifically to the disabled population. This further limits employment opportunities for people whose disabilities are more severe (Levitan and Taggart, 1977).

People with disabilities are generally at the end of the labor queue, and although they are more likely to be old, black, poor, and uneducated, even within these groups, disabled people are more likely to be unemployed (Levitan and Taggart, 1977). A recent unemployment figure for people with disabilities is 7.7 million (Bliss, 1982), and when they are employed, disabled people earn 70 percent of what able-bodied people do, securing 66 percent of the income (Levitan and Taggart, 1977, p. ix). A small number of sketchy data are available about the economic status of persons with amputations specifically. Nine percent of Americans without at least one major extremity have incomes above $25,000 a year. Forty-two percent earn less than $10,000, and almost 50 percent have fewer than nine years of formal education (Rehab Group, Inc., 1979, pp. 6–7). On the other hand, investigators found that, in 1969, approximately 84 percent of persons with above-elbow amputations fitted with a replacement prosthesis over a two-year period were employed (Davies et al., 1970, p. 35). The study did not measure income.

Specific characteristics of the disabled person bode ill or well for his or her rehabilitation. Researchers have compiled a list of factors related to adaptive behavioral responses to disability, and these include the nature and degree of functional limitation, the visibility of the impairment, and the related stigma, including responsibility imputed to the impaired person for the loss (Melvin and Nagi, 1970). Positive relationships were also found between rehabilitative success and youth, intelligence, education, and field independence (a psychological term denoting active organization of one's experience, complex defense mechanisms, and a well-defined body concept and sense of identity) (Anderrson and Berg, 1975). Persons with upper-extremity amputations generally exhibit two additional characteristics positively associated with rehabilitation: impairment that is musculoskeletal and not neurological, circulatory, or respiratory, and residual capabilities that are less difficult to determine and stabilize over time (Nagi, 1969).

The Rehabilitation Process

Virtually every person with an amputation is inducted into a rehabilitation process, a set of activities that are designed to produce adaptive behavior in individuals with disabilities. Help in learning new behaviors comes from physicians, psychologists, physical and occupational therapists, social workers, rehabilitation engineers, and in the case of people with amputations, prosthetists. Each of these professionals focuses on the adjustment of the disabled person to his or her changed life circumstances, and meeting with the rehabilitation team is really the first compensatory measure the person with an amputation takes.

Rehabilitation rests on two norms: the value placed on the dignity and independence, especially the economic independence, of the individual; and the desire to maintain order by suppressing deviance of any kind, including physical impairment (Rabinowitz and Mitsos, 1964). One social welfare theorist suggests that our protective response to the young, and by extension other dependents, is part of a genetic inheritance, although he admits that as dependency is institutionalized, our responses to it become warped (Gaylin, 1978). In psychoanalytic terms, rehabilitation brings the individual out of the partial psychological regression that results from functional loss, and mutual trust between the professional and his client serves as the foundation on which the client's identity is rebuilt. Learning theory casts rehabilitation as a reinforcement schedule that rewards behaviors identified as "independent." A sociocultural perspective reminds rehabilitation theorists that dependence is, at least to some extent, socially defined (Goldin et al., 1972); rehabilitation workers must therefore be sensitive to the social context in which the client lives and in which his or her independence will be manifested and observed.

The rehabilitation process has been defined as having three stages. First, illness or "disequilibrium" becomes apparent to the potential client, who is likely to have a cultural bias against asking for and receiving help. In the pre-client phase, the disabled individual explores the possibility of a helping relationship with a professional or agency, eventually taking up the sick role and a set of mutual expectations with the helper. Dependence characterizes the client stage, toward the end of which "reconstruction"—that is, increased activity and independence—is achieved. Finally, "social reintegration" occurs. The former client is now maximally autonomous and has modified his or her reference group without imputing inferiority to him or herself or to other people with disabilities. The product of the rehabilitation process is an "armamentarium of social skills, job potentials, energy-directing mechanisms, compensatory techniques and psychological armor" (Rabinowitz and Mitsos, 1964, p. 12). Hardware is sometimes found among the compensatory techniques.

Rehabilitation as it is now practiced developed in response to World War II and the polio epidemic of the 1940s and 1950s. Advanced traumatology together with the use of motorized vehicles for battlefield evacuation greatly increased the survival rate of seriously impaired soldiers. Large numbers of these men were housed in Veterans Administration hospitals, and the staff who treated them had the opportunity to become rehabilitation experts (and devotees of compensatory technology) (Corcoran, 1981). Soon after the war, the Committee on Prosthetics Research and Development of the National Research Council was formed to promote limb prosthetics research. The concept of an inter-professional clinic team emerged from the deliberations of this body, and post-amputation prosthetics education programs allowed easy introduction of the teamwork concept into the curriculum. By 1960 the concept was featured in programs at three major universities (Stewart and Bernstock, 1977). The rehabilitation literature continues to call for a multi-disciplinary approach.

The physician is one, and usually the ranking, member of the rehabilitation team. He or she may be a surgeon, an orthopedist, or a neurologist, and is increasingly likely to be a physiatrist—that is, a specialist in physical medicine and rehabilitation. Physiatry became a board-certified medical specialty in 1948; in 1982 there were about two thousand specialists in the United States (interview with physiatrist). The physiatrist is, among other things, a broker for rehabilitation technology. He or she advises the patient about what to buy and in some cases prescribes it. Unlike other physicians, the specialist in physical medicine focuses on functioning rather than cure. His or her primary concern is functional loss—a condition that gets comparatively little medical attention and that calls for a participating rather than passive patient (Wessen, 1965); one physiatrist interviewed for this study reported that, although he is required to prescribe assistive devices paid for under the Medicaid program, he generally signs off on the self-prescriptions of his more knowledgeable patients. Surgeons may also serve as leaders of rehabilitation teams, but critics claim that they are unwilling or unable to attend to long-term treatment especially when, as with amputation, the need for rehabilitation represents a surgical "failure" (Kerstein, 1980; Whipple, 1980). Many surgeons now refer their patients to physical medicine specialists, sometimes before surgery, so that the physiatrist can make equipment-related recommendations for the surgical procedure (interview with physiatrist).

The physical or occupational therapist is a second member of the clinic team. Traditionally, persons with lower-extremity amputations work with physical therapists and those with upper-extremity amputations work with occupational therapists, but both therapists train the patient to execute tasks under his or her changed life circumstances. Their objective is to help the patient to recover as much functioning as possible, especially the day-to-day functioning that is necessary for independent living. Technology may or may not be part of a rehabilitative regimen. When it is, the therapist evaluates client performance before and after introduction of the device. Observers disagree about the capacity of physical and occupational therapists for increased participation in the use of rehabilitation technologies. Two rehabilitation engineers interviewed separately reported that most therapists, especially younger ones, are interested in incorporating sophisticated technologies into their practice. Ideas for design modification will sometimes originate with a therapist, and an engineer who teaches a design course for occupational therapy students believes that they will be technically adept with assistive devices and sensitive to demands on teammates who do technical work (interview). Some therapists, however, seem to reject the integration of compensatory equipment into the rehabilitation process. According to some of their clients and teammates (interviews with team members and clients), they express a desire for direct physical contact with the client. Moreover, some technologies, like electric wheelchairs, appear to these professionals to be self-indulgent of people with disabilities. Many clients have complained that their therapists demand all of their physical energy, leaving them too exhausted to attend to other aspects of their lives (interviews with disabled individuals).

Many rehabilitation teams include a social worker, or similar professional, whose job is to link the team with extra-hospital benefit systems, including those that deliver and pay for compensatory technologies (interviews with clinic team leader; Murdoch and Hughes, 1973). Social workers may also serve as counselors who facilitate the client's adjustment to disability. As in social work generally, self-determination is the ultimate goal of rehabilitative counseling, but client self-determination may be difficult to achieve in a rehabilitation clinic setting. Social workers function in the context of the agency that employs them, and hospitals, which are primarily medical facilities, are likely to have norms and policies reflecting the patient's more passive role in acute care. Moreover, the social worker may find the aspirations of the rehabilitant unrealistic, either overblown or too restrained (Soyer, 1963). The introduction of rehabilitation technology focuses these issues. Are clients using the most powerful machines? Do they expect too much of them? Do they expect too much of themselves?

Prosthetists join the clinic team when the loss to be mitigated is

that of a limb. They play a major role in choosing and fitting a prosthesis. Originally practiced by armorers (Murdoch and Hughes,
1973), by dentists (Wilson, 1969), and by persons with amputations
fitting themselves (Stewart and Bernstock, 1977), prosthetics has
evolved over centuries. For reasons already stated, World War II
stimulated the professionalization of prosthetics, and the way in
which prosthetists were trained and consequently viewed began to
change. Earlier prosthetists were as concerned about the appearance
of artificial limbs as about their functioning. In the 1950s, however,
the National Research Council became committed to a broader scientific base for prosthetics practice and catalyzed federal funding of
courses at a small number of universities. Classroom instruction has
expanded since then and certification, granted by the American
Board of Certification in Prosthetics and Orthotics, requires appren-
ticeship and a written and practical examination (interviews with
prosthetists). Certification is not required everywhere, but some
manufacturers and hospitals recognize certified prosthetists only
(Theta Technology Corp., 1981; Fulford and Hall, 1968).

Most prosthetists work in relatively small firms, or "shops,"
where artificial limbs are constructed, often from components produced by large manufacturers, and where full-fledged prosthetists
sometimes retain fabrication technicians for the less demanding aspects of limb-making. Hospital clinics are another site of prosthetics
practice, but for the most part, rehabilitation-team prosthetists serve
in that capacity only part time, returning to their shops in the in-
terim. Prosthetists were consistently criticized by people interviewed
for this study. They were faulted by their clients for doing poor fittings and by rehabilitation engineers for being unimaginative. They
were sometimes said to resist technological progress. But prosthetists practice under two constraints. First, there are too few trained
professionals and not enough qualified technicians. The Rehabilitation Services Administration estimates that the client-to-prosthetist
ratio in this country is 500:1 (LaRocca and Turem, 1978, p. 63), and
surely this accounts for some of the poor fittings. A second problem,
especially for older prosthetists, is that their craft has experienced a
rapid infusion of electrical engineering problems. The Boston Elbow, for example, uses a microcomputer and must be fitted to allow

for reception and transmission of electromyographic signals. Still, prosthetists have come to work well with plastics, and high technology components are profitable as well as inevitable (interviews with prosthesis designer and prosthetists). Still some designers take care to build new prosthetic technology on principles with which prosthetists are already familiar (interviews with two prosthetics engineers).

When the rehabilitation client's disability does not result from amputation, a rehabilitation engineer may play the prosthetist's role on the clinic team. Wheelchairs and communications aids are two of the technologies team engineers may customize for individual clients. Rehabilitation engineering, like other rehabilitation specialties, dates from World War II. The physicians and engineers of the Committee on Prosthetics Research and Development (CPRD) met repeatedly during the 1950s to discuss the improvement of prosthetics practice. Eventually orthopedists were convinced of the relevance of engineering to the principles of the human body, and some engineers added physiology and medical science to their expertise. Rehabilitation engineering became a distinct specialty in about 1965 (interview with rehabilitation engineer), but there is not yet a consensus about the exact nature of the field. It resembles biomedical engineering, but rehabilitation engineers stress that they deal exclusively with external devices, never with life and death (interviews). The Rehabilitation Engineering Society of North America (RESNA) includes manufacturers and physical therapists as well as trained engineers. One of the original members of CPRD has stated that no one earns the title of rehabilitation engineer unless "he has wheelchair grease under his fingernails" (interview with RESNA official).

In interviews conducted for this study, rehabilitation engineers were said by others to have the wrong frame of mind for working with disability; they were faulted for being too much like engineers. The classic engineering approach to a problem is to identify it and define it quantitatively, to design a solution and expect it to be unambiguous (Dorf, 1974). Tracy Kidder echoes Richard C. Dorf when he says that engineers are most comfortable in a world "in which right and wrong answers exist. It's a binary world" (Kidder,

1981, p. 146). But problems of functional loss are rarely binary. They are messy—ambiguous, subjective, varying widely by individual and over time. And even the more traditional engineering problems necessitate trade-offs. Values like safety, reliability, and economy, for example, often compete, and the solution that is reached is a compromise. The complaints against rehabilitation engineers, then, are that they are unaware of the values they design into their machines or that the values they choose are the wrong ones.

Nowhere are these values questions more pronounced than in interactions between engineers and people with disabilities. High technology solutions, especially elegant ones, are likely to be more interesting to engineers than low technologies are. And some designers resent the disabled person's attempt to modify a device or use it in an unanticipated way (interview with rehabilitation engineer). The head of a statewide disability rights group, who himself uses a wheelchair, asserted that many rehabilitation engineering efforts are "a technological rip-off" (interview). Is it really necessary, he wonders, to build a wheelchair that climbs stairs, or are engineers overly committed to mainstreaming? Is it impossible for them to live with other people's limitations? On the other hand, one rehabilitation engineer said he does not want to find himself "colluding with a limited image of what's possible" (interview). He sometimes confronts the issue directly, explaining to a client that he will do what he can, but only if he can be what he is: an engineer.

The Boston Elbow:
A Case Study

The Boston Elbow is a proportional myoelectric arm prosthesis. That is, it is an artificial arm, battery-powered and controlled by signals from the user's stump muscles, and it moves at more than one speed. The Boston Elbow looks like a whole arm. It extends from a wrist (to which various hooks and artificial hands can be attached) to an above-the-elbow socket, but only the elbow joint is capable of movement. In engineering terms, the arm has one degree of free-dom—that is, it produces one movement of the human arm, elbow flexion and extension. (Unless otherwise noted, information presented in the rest of this chapter comes from interviews with six participants in the Boston Elbow project.)

The Boston Elbow is one of several battery-powered elbow prostheses and one of two that are myoelectrically controlled. This means that electrodes located in the socket of the prosthesis detect on the surface of the wearer's skin electromyographic (EMG) signals during contraction of his or her stump muscles. The signals are then transmitted to and interpreted by an analog computer housed in the prosthesis, and the battery-powered motor "takes orders" from the computer to flex the elbow. Although any muscle can provide a myoelectric signal, the Boston Elbow is designed to respond to the movement of residual biceps and triceps muscles, precisely those muscles that would ordinarily flex and extend the joint. Control of this prosthesis is meant to replicate control of the user's natural elbow.

The Boston Elbow is also a proportional prosthesis. This means that it moves at speeds proportional to the intensity of the user's muscle contractions. Myoelectric control is not necessarily proportional. EMG signals may simply turn a prosthesis on and off, in which case muscle contractions above and below some threshold strength cause elbow movement to start and stop, but the wearer is unable to vary the speed of the device. Proportional control, on the other hand, exploits the fact that more intense muscle contraction produces an electric signal of greater magnitude. The relationship is a continuous one, and by contracting his or her stump muscles more or less intensely, the wearer of a proportional control prosthesis produces a full range of signal magnitudes and is thus able to move the arm at a full range of speeds.

Innateness was an explicit goal of the originators of the Boston Elbow, who sought to minimize what engineers call "mental work-load," the conscious mental activity required of the user. It was thought that a proportional myoelectric prosthesis would come as close as possible to recreating the intimacy of the relationship between the natural elbow and the rest of the body. In addition to the expectation that this would reduce the time and effort involved in training the user, proportional myoelectric control by residual arm muscles had a compelling engineering logic. It represented an interface of human and machine modeled as much as possible on the natural relationship of muscle and joint.

Claims for the innateness of myoelectric prostheses should be heard in context. One critic of the devices asserts that such expressions as "'control by thought' are widely inaccurate and confuse the issue" (McKenzie, 1969, p. 372). Although the Boston Elbow is a "bionic" elbow, six-million-dollar expectations will be dashed. The prosthesis does not improve on, and actually falls short of, its human counterpart. Still, a person fitted with a Boston Elbow flexes and extends the prosthesis in much the same way as he or she flexed and extended the lost arm.

A Brief History of the Boston Elbow

The Boston Elbow is a product of three Boston institutions: the Massachusetts Institute of Technology, the Massachusetts General Hospital, and the Liberty Mutual Insurance Company. M.I.T. mathematician Norbert Wiener proposed in the late 1940s that cybernetic theory be applied to prosthetic devices. Although German scientists also started work on a myoelectric limb at this time (Childress, 1973), Wiener is considered the "godfather" of the Boston Elbow (see, for example, Wiener, 1951). His thinking was undoubtedly influential in the development of what is sometimes referred to as a "cybernetic" limb prosthesis.

In 1961, Wiener suffered a broken hip and was hospitalized at the Massachusetts General Hospital. His orthopedic surgeon, Melvin Glimcher, also headed the amputee clinic at the Liberty Mutual Insurance Company, a major carrier of workers' compensation policies. Glimcher related to Wiener that his patients with below-elbow amputations were using prostheses to recover much of their lost functioning. Patients with above-elbow amputations, however, did not fare so well. Even with the most advanced body-powered prosthesis, a person with an above-elbow amputation had first to position and then to open or close the hook or artificial hand. The arm was built with a single cable that did not allow for simultaneous execution of these two functions, and the wearer had to make unnatural body movements that were both unattractive and inefficient. Shortly before Wiener's hospitalization, Glimcher had visited the Soviet Union, where he had observed a myoelectric hand prosthesis. He took advantage of Wiener's temporary disability to discuss with him the possibility of extending Soviet technology to a myoelectrically controlled elbow. Myoelectric control seemed to Glimcher less necessary for persons with below-elbow amputations, who could function well with conventional cable devices. As one collaborator on the Boston Elbow project explained, the Elbow was created to render the person with an above-elbow amputation more like his or her below-elbow counterpart—that is, to allow him or her to use a hook or hand more effectively.

Wiener encouraged Glimcher's interest in a myoelectric elbow and put him in touch with two M.I.T. professors, Amar Bose of the Electrical Engineering Department, and Robert Mann, a mechanical engineer. Mann, under whose tutelage two generations of Boston Elbows were to be designed, had done his early work on missile power systems, where his task had been to find a way to supply and store energy for small, light objects capable of rapid activation. The relevance of this work to externally powered artificial limbs was not lost on the American Orthotics and Prosthetics Association. Mann was appointed to their National Survey Committee in 1961.

In 1965, M.I.T. produced two graduate theses about how a myoelectric elbow prosthesis might be achieved. Ralph Alter, a doctoral student under Professor Bose, concerned himself primarily with direct nervous system control of prosthetic devices. He concluded that, while this was not yet feasible, myoelectric control might be attempted. The second student, Ronald Rothchild, who was working with Professor Mann, brought to the elbow project a designer's perspective and completed a feasibility study for a myoelectrically controlled elbow prosthesis. Innateness was the distinct advantage of the Rothchild arm over conventional prostheses: it tapped the wearer's own muscles for flexion and extension. The hypothetical wearer could also support the weight of objects he or she wished to carry with the artificial limb. It was "a system in which the operator is required to flex his muscle and provide an EMG input to hold an external load. This approximates the situation with a normal arm" (Rothchild, 1965, p. 16).

Both Alter and Rothchild received research support from the Liberty Mutual Insurance Company, and in 1966, the firm hired two of Mann's former students, electrical engineer Cord Ohlenbusch and mechanical engineer David Russell, to build a real Boston Elbow. In 1968, Ohlenbusch and Russell did produce a myoelectic elbow prosthesis. The device was controlled by EMG signals from the wearer's stump processed by a computer housed in the artificial forearm. The Ohlenbusch-Russell arm was the Boston Elbow Version I. It debuted in the fall of 1968 at a press conference and exhibition at the Massachusetts General Hospital.

In 1969, Liberty Mutual signed a production agreement with EG&G, Inc., a local electronics firm that manufactured eighteen Ohlenbusch-Russell arms over a two-year period. The project was by all accounts a failure: almost every person fitted with the prosthesis rejected it, and a National Research Council evaluation found EG&G's product to be unsatisfactory (LeBlanc, 1971). A consultant to the Boston Elbow project cited managerial problems at EG&G—difficulty procuring the right equipment and parts and the dread not-invented-here syndrome—in explaining the early flop. Other participants emphasized that the EG&G arm came with a battery so large it had to be mounted on the wearer's belt. This, in the words of one engineer, was "no fun."

Robert Jerard, a mechanical engineering student under Mann, wrote a 1970 thesis offering an elbow mechanism so compact that a wrist rotator and hand could be added to the prosthesis. Liberty Mutual then hired Jerard to transfer this technology from the university to the firm (Jerard et al., 1974), where Ohlenbusch had by this time reduced the energy consumption of the Elbow by refining its electronics. Jerard's subsequent replacement with a clutch of the Elbow's electrically operated brake made it possible for the battery to sit in the prosthetic forearm. Five Jerard arms were built during his one-year stay at Liberty Mutual. In 1973, a production engineer named T. Walley Williams was brought to the firm to modify Jerard's Elbow for in-house manufacture, and in 1974, Williams produced twenty-five working Boston Elbows, many of which were still being worn in the early 1980s. Liberty Mutual manufactured one hundred improved Elbows in 1976. Some of these have yet to be purchased. Another one hundred arms have been recently constructed.

At its current stage of development, the Boston Elbow is a proportional myoelectric elbow prosthesis. Ideally, the wearer's stump has intact biceps and triceps muscles. If not, appropriate muscle sites can be located elsewhere and the wearer trained to use these muscles to flex and extend his or her elbow. The stump is fitted for a socket resembling the socket of a conventional prosthesis, but the Boston Elbow features electrodes that detect and transmit electromyographic signals produced by stump-muscle contraction. An electronics component housed in the forearm of the prosthesis processes and interprets these signals and communicates to the motor how fast and in what direction the elbow should move. This is the cybernetic aspect of the Boston Elbow. The device's electronics consist of an analog computer, chosen over the now more common digital machine because the information transmitted is not encoded but rather a continuous variable. The motor is powered by rechargeable nickel-cadmium batteries, also housed in the forearm, that power about eight hours of moderate use or two hours of heavy use before recharging is necessary. In about fifteen minutes, the batteries can be recharged to 85 percent of their full strength, but if the residual 15 percent is not attended to regularly, the capacity of the device for eight hours' use will shrink.

Fitting a Boston Elbow requires the participation of both prosthetist and user, and the prosthesis is engineered to facilitate the involvement of both. The upper-arm socket, for example, is much like the one fitted for a conventional device. The prosthetist makes a cast of the stump and then a mold to which socket material is fitted. When he or she has built from the socket to the elbow with layers of foam, the prosthetist attaches an elbow unit consisting of motor, reverse-locking clutch, and speed reduction gearing. The forearm houses batteries, electronics, and the recharge connector, and it is noticeably boxy-looking, especially on a woman.

The Boston Elbow offers the user a choice of terminal devices. He or she may choose a conventional—that is, cable-operated— hook or hand controlled by the opposing shoulder or a hook or hand operated with an electric or myoelectric shoulder switch. The elbow prosthesis is designed so that hook and hand are interchangeable and may be used by the same wearer at different times. The Boston Elbow weighs 2.5 pounds and it lifts 4.5. It has a maintenance cycle of something over a year and a service life of about five years. The elbow unit sells for $5,000, but in order to wear it, a person must also have a socket, fitting, and training. The estimated cost of these additions is $7,500, bringing the full cost of the Boston Elbow to $12,500.

Current Research in Myoelectric Prosthetics

The Boston Elbow has spawned two major, and divergent, research efforts, both of them through mechanical engineering students under Robert Mann. In 1973, Stephen Jacobsen proposed in his doctoral thesis that the electromyographic activity of groups of shoulder muscles be used to provide additional functions, additional "degrees of freedom," in an arm prosthesis. Whereas the Boston Elbow tapped muscles that controlled the intact elbow joint, Jacobsen was addressing the need for functions—for example, rotation of the forearm—that required amputated muscles or muscles recruited for flexion and extension.

Jacobsen based his design strategy on the characteristics of muscles around the shoulder girdle. These, it was found, "anticipate" what more distant joints—for example, the wrist—are about to do. The shoulder muscles can even be said to "orchestrate" the movement of a distant joint and the accompanying movement of the surrounding anatomy. Therefore, electrodes detecting EMG signals in shoulder muscles can transmit information about the intended functioning of another joint. This became the logic of Jacobsen's prosthesis. His arm could hypothetically control as many degrees of freedom as muscle sites could be involved.

At the conclusion of his doctoral research, Jacobsen undertook to refine and develop the prosthesis he had designed at M.I.T., the Utah Arm, as it would come to be called. Jacobsen concerned himself not only with building an innate and functional machine but with conceiving a second-generation device that would be relatively easy to manufacture and market (Jacobsen et al., 1982). For example, the Utah Arm is actually a set of component parts, a series of modules that give the prosthesis five degrees of freedom: grasp, wrist articulation, elbow flexion and extension, forearm rotation, and shoulder movement. At present the hand, wrist, and elbow are powered; the other joints are passive, manipulatable by the opposing hand. Jacobsen's long-term objective is to provide a complete range of interchangeable parts—from shoulder to hand, and passive, body-powered, and myoelectric. The wearer of the Utah Arm will thus be able to combine modules as impairment, purpose, and taste dictate. A modular device also minimizes repair and replacement problems.

The design of the Utah Arm calls for a digital, rather than an analog, computer. Jacobsen envisions a prosthesis with variable functions—that is, a machine that can function in different ways with a change in software—and this kind of variability is not possible with an analog processor. Again, the Utah Arm is designed for versatility. This both broadens its appeal and lowers the anticipated costs of retooling for improved prostheses. The first Utah Arm was fitted in 1981.

Another of Mann's students was Neville Hogan, who has remained at M.I.T. to direct further work on myoelectric arm prostheses. Whereas Jacobsen's research aims at increasing the number of degrees of freedom available in the myoelectric prosthesis, Hogan addresses the problem of positioning a device without sensory feedback. Mann calls sensory feedback—information about the prosthesis' force or position communicated to the wearer—the "most refractory" problem in myoelectric prosthetic engineering (Mann, 1981). A conventional prosthesis provides some feedback to the shoulder that controls elbow movement, but this information is minimized in the myoelectric prosthesis, which does not involve the shoulder joint. Visual and sometimes auditory feedback are produced when a Boston Elbow is used, but these provide insufficient information to close the system's "open loop," and the wearer's physical coordination is easily disrupted. Calls for better sensory input are common. Poor feedback is cited as a major reason for low rates of acceptance of externally powered prostheses (e.g. Korner, 1979; McKenzie, 1969), and engineers propose the use of mechanical vibration or electric stimulation for feedback from these devices (Childress, 1973; Mann and Reimers, 1970). Hogan takes issue with the emphasis on feedback. He does not believe that it is the lack of sensory input that makes externally pow‑ ered prostheses difficult to position, nor that improvement of myo‑ electric elbows lies with a capacity for feedback. Hogan argues in‑ stead that users of the Boston Elbow suffer from its rigidity. It is not, in Hogan's words, "floppy" or "springy" and so does not respond as the natural arm does—by adapting its force to that of other objects. Hogan draws heavily on his work with physiologist Emilio Bizzi (Bizzi et al., 1980). Bizzi, who studies neural control, has found that, when a monkey has been trained to point to a visual target, he will continue to do so even without sensory feedback. Presumably this occurs because his muscles have inherent mechanical impedance characteristics, such as force, stiffness, and viscosity. The brain "counts on" these properties to maintain the position of the limb when the environment changes, and the muscles spring back. Hogan interprets Bizzi's findings to mean that sensory feedback is not criti‑ cal for a prosthetic arm. If the prosthesis is given the same impedance characteristics as the natural limb, it will adapt to changes in the en‑ vironment even without sensory input. Hogan suggests that what‑ ever feedback capacities are developed for prosthetic limbs be used for sensation in the fingers where such information is crucial to per‑ formance (interview).

Prosthetic Alternatives to the Boston Elbow

There are three major prosthetic alternatives to the Boston El‑ bow. In order of technical sophistication they are the conventional body-powered elbow prosthesis, the switch-controlled electric el‑ bows, and another myoelectric, proportional arm. Each can be found in a small prosthetics market, where five firms account for 95 percent of the sales, and sales to prosthetists were an estimated $31 million in 1981. About 55 percent, or $17 million, was spent on upper-ex‑ tremity prostheses, although less costly lower-extremity devices were bought in larger numbers. An estimated $5 million was spent on above-elbow prostheses in 1981 (Theta Technology Corp., 1981, pp. 1, 51, 53).

Table 1. ELBOW PROSTHESES

FEATURES	BOSTON ELBOW	CABLE ELBOW	NYU-HOSMER ELBOW	VA ELBOW	UTAH ARM (ELBOW)
Power	battery	body	battery	battery	battery
Control	myoelectric	musculoskeletal movement	switch	switch	myoelectric
Proportional	yes	yes	no	no	yes
No. of powered joints	1	0	1	1	1
Weight	2.5 lbs.	15 oz.	1 lb.	1+ lbs.	2 lbs. 1 oz.
Lift	4.5 lbs.	2 lbs.	3.5 lbs.	3 lbs.	2 + lbs.
Hold	50 lbs.	50 lbs.	20 lbs.	10 lbs.	50 lbs.
Speed	1 sec.	1 sec.	1.2 secs.	1.5 secs.	.64 secs.
Range	145°	135°	130°	135°	135°
Free swing	30°	total	total	120°	total
Repair cycle	1/yr.	1/yr.	1/yr.	1.5/yr.	2/yr.
Repair local	some	yes	some	some	some
Time w/o recharge	8 hrs.	—	18 hrs.	8 hrs.	10 hrs.*
Full recharge time	2 hrs.	—	8 hrs.	2 hrs.	16 hrs.
Cost†	$5,000	$300	$1,500	$900	$10,700

Note: Data for arms from personal communications with manufacturers and participating engineers. All data are approximations. Experts disagree about the importance of these features.
*But immediately replaceable.
†To prosthetist for elbow alone.

The body-powered elbow is the oldest and most frequently worn of the above-elbow prostheses. It is designed with a steel cable running the length of the arm, and the wearer rolls his or her shoulder to flex the elbow. A body-powered prosthesis is not an innate device. It requires unnatural shoulder movement on the part of the user and does not permit elbow and terminal device to operate at the same time. Because the prosthesis is powered by the user, it is less powerful than prostheses with batteries and less efficient for lifting and holding. On the other hand, the cable-operated arm is lighter than most externally powered devices (see Table 1), and weight is an important consideration for most wearers. A conventional elbow is also virtually noiseless and has a relatively long maximum life. Its cost is about $300. The Hosmer Dorrance Corporation sells the largest number of body-powered elbows. It is the second largest firm in the prosthetics market, with earnings of $7 million in 1981 (Theta Technology Corp., 1981, p. 1). Hosmer also began to market a switch-controlled electric elbow, the NYU-Hosmer Elbow, in 1983 (personal communication with Hosmer official).

All commercially available externally powered elbows are electric—that is, they run on batteries. The means of controlling these prostheses differ, however. The switches found on the Veterans Administration (VA) Elbow (sometimes called the VA Prosthetics Center or VAPC Elbow), for example, are less sophisticated than the Boston Elbow's myoelectric control mechanism. The wearer of a pull- or push-switch prosthesis can turn it on and off with slight shoulder movement and he or she enjoys all the advantages of an externally powered device. The VA and NYU-Hosmer Elbows also weigh less than the Boston Elbow (again see Table 1), but the first two are not proportional and move at one relatively slow speed. Neither are they as strong as the Boston Elbow. The cost of the VA elbow is $900. It was designed at the VA but was manufactured until 1985 by Fidelity Electronics, the third largest manufacturer of upper-extremity devices. Fidelity earned an estimated $4 million in the manufacture of limbs in 1981 (Theta Technology Corp., 1981, p. 1), although the company has discontinued production of the VA Elbow due to its poor market share. The price of the NYU Elbow, which can be converted by a prosthetist to myoelectric switch control is $1,500 (personal communication with participating engineer.)

The Utah Arm is the only commercially available proportional myoelectric alternative to the Boston Elbow. It is, as noted above, a progeny of the Boston Elbow. The Utah Arm's elbow unit costs $10,700 alone and an average of $20,000 fitted to the wearer. For additional details consult Table 1.

Myoelectric Prostheses Considered

In 1961, Melvin Glimcher approached Robert Mann and Amar Bose about building a myoelectric prosthesis for above-elbow amputations. Over one hundred people are wearing this elbow, and for them, as Glimcher had hoped, elbow flexion and operation of the hook or hand are independent and simultaneous. There are, however, approximately 50,000 Americans with above-elbow amputations, and obstacles to further diffusion of the Boston Elbow are hypothesized in several ways. The more political arguments will be discussed in later chapters, but some critics find fault with the actual design of the Boston Elbow or with the way in which the design is perceived by potential users.

Externally powered arm prostheses, including the Boston Elbow, are widely considered to have undesirable qualities; their heaviness, slowness, noisiness, and need for battery recharging lead many potential users to favor a cable-operated device or no prosthesis at all (Abul-Haj and Hogan, 1981; also interviews with physicians and prosthetists). The Committee on Prosthetics Research and Development evaluated three electrically powered elbows in 1969 (LeBlanc, 1971), and the Boston Elbow was among the prostheses tested by twenty-one persons with amputations, seventeen of whom preferred the body-powered elbows to any electric one. CPRD concluded that externally powered arms were not ready for general use and that the most the committee could do was issue a set of standards to guide further development of these devices. Weight, speed, and noise were among CPRD's concerns, as was a better appearance. Even now, those working on the Boston Elbow admit that the forearm is too square and hard to offer much cosmesis, and while the elbow unit itself weighs only 2.5 pounds, the complete arm prosthesis weighs more than four (interviews). (The human arm weighs approximately ten pounds, but a prosthesis is always perceived by the wearer to be heavier.)

One investigator found statistically significant differences in the acceptance rates of a myoelectric hand prosthesis by persons with below-elbow amputations, when the experimental group was trained to use the device and the control group was not. He interpreted this to mean that, whereas trained users may reject a myoelectric prosthesis, untrained users almost certainly will (Herberts et al., 1980). It should be pointed out that a myoelectric below-elbow prosthesis is not as innate, and therefore not as easy to use, as a Boston Elbow controlled by biceps and triceps muscles. Still, some percentage of Boston Elbow wearers do not have sufficiently intact biceps and triceps and so must learn to use other muscles to control the elbow joint. The need for training might be considered a disadvantage of myoelectric prostheses, but persons with amputations must learn to use even the simplest cable elbow.

Officials at the Massachusetts Rehabilitation Commission, the National Institute of Handicapped Research (NIHR), and the Rehabilitation Services Administration (interviews) charged that the Boston Elbow is unnecessarily "high" technology. They argued that research in myoelectric prosthetics is theoretical and esoteric, "so technical," according to one disabled rehabilitation professional, that it yields only "fancy devices" that are difficult to use. These officials agreed about the source of the problem: M.I.T., like other academic settings, is simply inappropriate to prosthetics research. Engineers in university laboratories, it was argued, are motivated to produce theses not prostheses. Taking a slightly different position, an engineer at NIHR raised issues of marginal utility. For him the Boston Elbow is "essentially overkill"—that is, unnecessarily complex technology at a price much greater than that of an adequate alternative. He acknowledged that the Elbow out-performs other prostheses, but concluded that this advantage does not warrant the difference in its price. And doubts about marginal utility extend to the Utah Arm, which was described as "beautiful engineering," the diffusion of which is "going to be a disaster" (interview).

Proponents of the Boston Elbow responded to these and other criticisms by asserting that a proportional myoelectric prosthesis is qualitatively better than its alternatives. It is considered, for reasons discussed above, to be more innate and therefore substantially easier for the user to operate. One Liberty Mutual official argued that this in turn encourages its users to undertake new tasks, to expand their activity and mastery. As for marginal utility, he admitted that, at least in some instances, it may be small, but he pointed out that this is a very individual calculus and one that varies over the lifetime of the user (interviews).

Another response from the myoelectric camp was that, although for some the marginal utility of the Boston Elbow is modest, there are others for whom it is one of few workable prostheses. Persons with high above-elbow and shoulder disarticulation amputations, for example, cannot be fitted with conventional cable-operated elbows. In the past, these individuals became "one-armed." They adapted their behavior to being without the lost limb and in many cases found environmental substitutes for it: a paperweight, for example, will secure writing paper on a desk. A single hand will open a jar held between one's knees.

The Boston Elbow is of course not suited to every person with an above-elbow or even high above-elbow amputation. One prosthetist interviewed noted that, for obvious reasons, new prostheses claim universal applicability but seldom manifest it. In the case of the Boston Elbow, the user must be willing to attend to its electric power. Batteries for the prosthesis will run down after about eight hours and must be fully recharged if they are to retain an eight-hour capacity. Moreover, the user must keep track of how much time remains on any charge; the prosthetic arm will stop moving— possibly in a undesirable position—when the power runs out.

According to a 1981 overview of the prosthetics field (Peizer, 1981), myoelectric control is one of six areas in which technological change can be expected. Mann is "confident that all of the really significant technological problems of adequate prostheses . . . are achievable, . . . limited only by the financial and manpower resources brought to bear" (Mann, 1973, p. 73). Another engineer speaks for many when he says: "The most positive aspect of powered prostheses is the promise they hold for the future" (Childress, 1973, p. 202).

In the chapters that follow, three classes of people with amputations and their compensatory options will be discussed at length. Many of the issues raised in this chapter will be reiterated in relation to the particular social welfare systems that shape government's response to functional loss. The framework for understanding public diffusion of the Boston Elbow will organize and elucidate the sets of options to which the classes of people with amputations are entitled. The Boston Elbow will appear as an alternative in a set of options offered by government to redress functional loss.

2
Bearing Arms
The Veteran

Veterans are among those to whom government diffuses compensatory technology. The Veterans Administration (VA) researches, builds, buys, and distributes these devices. In 1980, about 4,600 veterans were receiving service-connected disability compensation for the loss of one or both upper extremities. An estimated 100 of them were wearing externally powered elbow prostheses (personal communication with VA official), but few individuals fitted through the VA system wear a Boston Elbow (interviews with VA and Liberty Mutual officials). This chapter will describe and analyze the compensatory array of the veteran with an above-elbow amputation (see Figure 3). It is a generous array, although the Boston Elbow was added only in 1985 (interview with VA official). That the Elbow was for many years not diffused through the VA reveals something about public distribution of compensatory technology: diffusion of any one device must be viewed in the context of other benefits— technological and not.

In the case of the veteran, the Boston Elbow was not diffused in a more timely way for two reasons. First, the Veterans Administration offers its own externally powered elbow prosthesis: the VA Elbow. Less sophisticated than the Boston Elbow, the VA's prosthesis is not myoelectrically controlled. It is, as noted above, electrically powered and controlled by means of a switch at the wearer's shoulder. Once the wearer activates the device, the VA Elbow runs at a constant speed—that is, the speed at which the arm operates is not proportional to the muscle activity of the wearer. Still, the VA's prosthesis competes with the Boston Elbow for use by persons with above-elbow amputations for whom an externally powered device is suitable.

The second reason the Boston Elbow has not diffused through the veterans system is that the veteran with an amputation is entitled not only to a prosthesis but to a large set of compensatory options. Compensation for service-connected amputation in particular includes some form of every measure in the contextual framework. An externally powered prosthesis is only one of the benefits provided to help the veteran cope with armlessness; it is reasonable to think, given the limited usefulness of any prosthesis, that some of the alternatives to artificial arms might enjoy a comparative advantage. The veterans system has been slow to diffuse the Boston Elbow not because it skimps on compensation but because it offers so many compensatory alternatives.

Prosthetics in the Veterans System

The Role of the VA in Prosthetics Research and Development

War punctuates the history of American prosthetics. Prior to World War I, artificial limbs were produced by independent craftsmen, many of whom themselves had had amputations. Prosthetists organized as a profession in 1917, when a group of them was summoned by the surgeon general of the army to consider problems of the World War I wounded. The Association of Limb Manufacturers of America, known today as the American Orthotics and Prosthetics Association (AOPA), was formed in the aftermath of this meeting (Stewart and Bernstock, 1977).

At the end of World War II, the army's surgeon general again took up the cause of the disabled veteran, this time on behalf of the approximately 25,000 soldiers who lost a limb in the war (Wilson, 1969, p. 209). Many of these veterans were dissatisfied with the prostheses available to them, and the surgeon general relayed their complaints to the National Academy of Sciences (NAS). NAS responded by convening a discussion of the state of American prosthetics. There the opinion was voiced that existing prostheses suffered from insufficient science—that is, that prosthetists were treating clients from an inadequate knowledge base. A joint committee of the National Research Council (NRC) and NAS, the Committee on Prosthetic Devices (later known as the Committee on Prosthetic Research and Development [CPRD]), was formed at this time to advance prosthetics research (Wilson, 1981; Stewart and Bernstock, 1977). One participant in this undertaking remembers the strong sense of possibility that motivated his colleagues. Not only did veterans hospitals furnish an adequately large pool of potential users, but VA professionals had great expectations of what research could do for America's fallen heroes (interview with VA rehabilitation engineer).

CPRD's strategy was to make research monies available to contracting universities and industries. Funds were provided briefly by the Office of Scientific Research and Development and then for many years by the Veterans Administration. The committee ultimately took on an advisory role and relinquished the actual contracting to the VA, which at about this time established its own prosthetics research and development laboratory in New York City. The CPRD/VA research effort remained a primary source of prosthetics science and design until CPRD disbanded in 1976 (Stewart and Bernstock, 1977; Wilson, 1981).

Research done under contract with the Veterans Administration included work on body- and externally powered prostheses, and the former were significantly improved during the 1950s. Lighter and more durable prostheses were constructed using a plastic laminate instead of wood and an adapted aircraft cable instead of a leather thong. Sockets were redesigned for user comfort; elbow joints were refashioned to lock in an increased number of positions. Investigators also focused on improving prosthetics research itself. For example, contractors at the University of California at Los Angeles developed a set of basic motion requirements for above-elbow prostheses. This was an attempt to standardize the criteria by which artificial arms would be evaluated in the future (Stewart and Bernstock, 1977; Theta Technology Corp., 1981).

The VA also funded research on externally powered arms. According to an engineer on the VA staff at the time, the desirability of external power was "obvious" to him and his colleagues: externally powered arms would execute movements with increased force and ease (interview). Samuel Alderson was one researcher who received long-term VA support. He was funded to realize in five models his idea for an electrically powered upper-extremity prosthesis.

Alderson's arm was battery-powered and featured a system of switches for applying power to several functions. The wearer operated the switches with shoulder and stump movement and was able in this way to achieve flexion at the shoulder, upper-arm rotation, elbow flexion and extension, forearm pronation and supination, wrist flexion, and hand articulation, each with a different switch. The first model of the Alderson arm was heavy and noisy, and even once problems of weight and noise had been solved, the prosthesis required enormous concentration and retained the robot-like appearance of all non-proportional devices. Alderson eventually redirected his efforts from a total prosthesis to prosthesis components (Stewart and Bernstock, 1977).

The Veterans Administration researched a myolectric elbow prosthesis, but chose to develop a switch-controlled device instead. An engineer who participated in this decision recalled its having been a choice between concentrating on myoelectric control and pursuing other desirable features, such as multiple degrees of freedom. The "innateness" of myoelectric control was thought to be less important than features that seemed incompatible with myoelectricity—self-containment, cosmesis, and quiet. As noted above, the earliest Boston Elbow featured a battery pack to be worn on the user's belt, because it was impossible to house both the power source and the electronics within the prosthetic forearm. For the same reason, the self-contained Boston Elbow is noticeably boxy and heavy relative to the VA's prosthesis. As the participating engineer put it, the VA Elbow forearm has "no guts"—it houses none of the sophisticated electronics that make the Boston Elbow a myoelectric device. Thus the VA Elbow can more closely resemble the human forearm in its contours (interview).

The VA Elbow was conceived in the mid-1960s and so was contemporaneous with the Boston Elbow and a number of now obsolete externally powered arm prostheses. Veterans began to use the VA Elbow in 1969, and like the Boston Elbow, it has been modified over time. The Veterans Administration does not manufacture equipment, so production of the VA Elbow has been contracted out to a series of private firms. The Elbow's second incarnation, achieved by the Hosmer Co. (now Hosmer Dorrance), was functional but unattractive and noisy. It is now in its third variation, and is sometimes fitted to non-veterans whose prosthetists order the Elbow directly from the manufacturer, Fidelity Electronics (interview with VA engineer).

The VA Elbow is among the lightest of the externally powered elbow prostheses, weighing little more than a body-powered device. Its appearance is also among the best, although the prosthesis' non-proportional speed lends it a robotic quality. As a switch-controlled device, the VA Elbow is activated and deactivated by the wearer's shoulder movement. It sells for about $900. Fidelity Electronics is primarily a manufacturer of hearing aids and computer games and contracted to make the VA Elbow after U.S. Manufacturing, maker of the first VA Elbow, and Hosmer decided not to continue their involvement. It is unlikely that the VA Elbow will be developed further, although the Veterans Administration is funding a number of projects related to externally powered prostheses (interviews at VA and Fidelity Electronics; Philipson et al., 1981).

VA prosthetics research and development is the province of three groups. The Rehabilitation Engineering Research and Development Service (RER&D) is charged with doing intramural research and development, contracting for work at other institutions, and establishing university-affiliated rehabilitation engineering programs (interview with RER&D official). In fiscal year 1981, RER&D sponsored approximately eighty projects and had a budget of over $8.5 million (OTA, 1981, p. 64). The group's mandate is to

develop any device or technique that will contribute to the rehabilitation of a disabled veteran (interview with RER&D official). The
scope of this work is broad, including both person- and environ-
ment-focused measures for veterans with, among other disabilities,
spinal-cord injuries, voice loss, and amputations. But mitigating the
effects of amputation was named by the same official as among
RER&D's highest priorities. He asserted a need for improved
prostheses and identified obvious knowledge gaps, such as how to
provide sensory feedback, that VA activity might be able to fill (interview). In fiscal year 1981, RER&D spent more than a million
dollars on prosthetics and orthotics research, not including an additional $1.5 million spent on improving amputation and other surgi-
cal procedures (OTA, 1982, p. 65). The director of RER&D also
chairs the editorial board of the *Journal of Rehabilitative Engineering
Research*, a quarterly publication that reaches professionals in all VA
amputee clinics.

The Veterans Administration Rehabilitation Engineering Center (VAREC) is technically part of RER&D, but for many years
VAREC acted as an autonomous body. The Center has a long history of clinical programs and evaluation research in addition to
research and development. It has also distributed rehabilitation
technologies to users throughout the veterans system. In 1981, the
VA's inspector general found the VAREC leadership to be guilty of
a misuse of funds (Feinsilber, 1981). A blue-ribbon committee was
established to review the Center's activities (including the purchase
of large numbers of electric hands that were never distributed), and
on the committee's recommendation, VAREC is being dismantled
and replaced with small, regional engineering teams (interview with
VAREC staff member and VA officials). Several of the people interviewed for this study saw the VAREC scandal as a generational matter, a deposing of old leaders by new. The outcome of most significance to the Boston Elbow was that the Center's long-time director
and his closest associates retired, leaving VAREC to the head of the
Prosthetic and Sensory Aids Service (PSAS). With this additional
authority, PSAS promptly approved distribution of the Boston Elbow, the Utah Arm, and the NYU-Hosmer Elbow through the VA
system (interview with PSAS official).

PSAS is the third participant in VA prosthetics research and development. Its small research agenda is entirely evaluative and derives from the agency's mandate to deliver high-quality prosthetic services to all eligible veterans. The PSAS evaluation and approval process will be described in the next section of this chapter.

Delivering Prosthetic Services
    Veterans receive prosthetic services through the Veterans Administration health care system. Established in its present form in 1946, this network of facilities was designed to allow maximum freedom for physicians who would in return provide superior care for the American veteran (Thompson, 1981). The veterans system has had an acute care orientation, but both physician and non-physician members of VA amputation clinic teams have reported physicians' growing interest in rehabilitation medicine (interviews). The Veterans Administration spent $816 million in 1977 for medical care related to disabling conditions. The corresponding figures for Medicare and Medicaid were $1.4 and $2.8 billion respectively (OTA, 1981, p. 103).
    The VA both fabricates and contracts for prosthetic devices. In fiscal year 1976, almost 9,000 artificial limbs were purchased from commercial vendors for eligible veterans, while another 2,000 were furnished by the VA directly. More than 650 of the new prostheses were upper-extremity devices; in the same year, almost as many arms were repaired (Stewart and Bernstock, 1977, pp. 10, 5, 6). PSAS spent a total of $93.5 million on prosthetics and sensory aids (including repairs) in fiscal year 1982 (VA, 1983, n.p.). The service is also responsible for the evaluation and approval of all devices provided to VA clients. As one official put it, he and his colleagues keep veterans from rolling backwards down hills in their wheelchairs (interview). PSAS approves prostheses on the basis of evaluations conducted by the agency or by another investigator. In the mid-1980s the service began to rely on manufacturers' own evaluations. Vendors as well as devices must have PSAS approval. In the case of prosthetists this means only certified practitioners will be paid to provide artificial limbs to veterans (interviews with PSAS officials and staff).

An as yet unapproved device can find its way to the veteran through either the regular PSAS evaluation process or a ruling by PSAS on an individual case. The former generally begins when the manufacturer of some rehabilitation technology contacts the service and requests that the product be considered for approval. A physician or prosthetist on a VA clinic team may also recommend a technology that has not yet been approved and ask PSAS to allow the device in an individual case (interview with VA staff). Presumably, items for which a significant number of requests have been made are considered for standard PSAS approval.

The Boston Elbow became a PSAS-approved prosthesis in early 1985. Some Veterans Administration officials interviewed for this study knew of no reason why the Elbow had not been approved sooner, unless perhaps that it was rarely prescribed. Liberty Mutual and other VA officials, however, claimed that the Boston Elbow was neither prescribed for VA clients nor PSAS-approved because the VA Elbow was automatically provided to a potential user instead. Even now, the VA Elbow retains the advantage of greater familiarity among VA staff and on-site repair at many VA clinics. An ailing Boston Elbow is usually returned to or replaced by Liberty Mutual's laboratory in Hopkinton, Massachusetts.

PSAS reaches the veteran through amputee clinic teams. Like the hypothetical team described in Chapter 1, the VA clinic team includes a physician, a physical/occupational therapist, and a prosthetist. The veteran with an amputation is also assigned a Prosthetics Representative who, like the hypothetical social worker, serves as a counselor and coordinates the rehabilitation effort. This position was created in 1946, at about the same time as the rehabilitation team concept, and Prosthetics Representatives were originally required to be disabled themselves and to be wearing a prosthetic device. The Prosthetics Representative embodies the ideal of a client-oriented, interdisciplinary approach to rehabilitation. He or she also focuses attention on the technological response to functional loss. Not only does the title reinforce the client's expectation that prosthetics will be at the center of his treatment, but the Prosthetics Representative position was actually designed to link local manufacturers and dealers to the veterans system and to provide technical assistance on prosthetics to clinic staff (Stewart and Bernstock, 1977).

Many VA amputee clinic teams include two prosthetists, one a VA employee and one a local practitioner. Both contribute to the decision to prescribe one or another prosthesis, and a third may ultimately provide the client with the device. Local prosthetists who are certified to practice are asked by the VA to serve, on a rotating basis, as consultants to the clinic team. The client may then take his or her prescription to any certified practitioner to be filled. Prosthetists are increasingly professionally organized, and as more of them achieve certification, the Veterans Administration has a larger pool of experts from which to draw. But one VA official notes that another aspect of professionalization is the appearance in many prosthetics shops of technicians who simply assemble prefabricated prosthetic components. The VA is troubled by this trend and requires that a full-fledged prosthetist do every fitting of every veteran's prosthesis. VA clinic staff are also trained to recognize inferior workmanship (interviews with VA officials and staff). There is expressed throughout the VA a commitment to fine hardware.

Recipients of Veterans Administration prosthetic services fall into two groups. The first comprises individuals whose amputations result from a service-connected injury or disease (that is, an injury or disease that first occurred while the individual was in the armed services) and those who are 50 percent or more disabled from a service-connected injury or disease and undergo amputation for some other reason. The second group includes veterans with non-service-connected amputations who are in-patients at VA hospitals and for whom a prosthesis is part of discharge planning (also veterans who served in the Spanish-American War or World War I, former prisoners of war, and veterans who are so disabled as to be receiving a grant for "aid and attendance"—that is, a personal care attendant). The second group of veterans are provided with a single prosthesis and receive replacement devices only if they continue to patronize VA facilities for repairs and adjustments. Persons in the first group are entitled to more generous benefits. They are provided with two prostheses, of the same or different types, services from a prosthetist of their choosing, and replacement of the devices when necessary. Members of the first group also receive an allowance of up to $300 a year to cover the replacement of clothing damaged by prostheses (interview with VA Prosthetics Representative).

Despite these distinctions, all veterans who are eligible for prosthetic services are treated by the same VA clinic teams, and their
mandate is to fit clients with the best possible prostheses. Devices are
chosen not only on the basis of level of amputation and condition
of the stump but in response to the user's life circumstances and
reportedly with his or her input. Should the team's judgment prove
incorrect or the client's preferences change over time, the client is expected to return to the clinic for another prescription (interview
with VA Prosthetics Representative). A physician who has served on
both VA and other clinic teams said that, even in treating veterans in
the second group, VA professionals are more ambitious than others.
He attributed this in part to the VA's larger in-house technical staff
but emphasized the unique relationship between veterans and the
professionals who care for them (interview). One Prosthetics Representative explained that VA clinic staff serve a unique and highly val-
ued client group and therefore try to serve them as well as possible
(interview). In addition, every VA hospital has a Veterans Service
Office, staffed by members of veterans groups. Here a dissatisfied client can find a volunteer advocate, an arrangement described by one
PSAS official as his "housing the enemy" (interview). According to
the physician cited above, the VA's highly organized system of advocates makes his job more difficult, but means better treatment for
veterans with amputations (interview).

The veteran with an amputation is eligible for prosthetic
services that are at least adequate, and in some cases generous. A
description of the veteran's prosthetic options, however, is an incomplete statement of his or her compensatory opportunities. Prosthetics are one response to loss of an arm, and the veterans system
provides the client with a full array.

Other Responses to Functional Loss

Look for a moment at Figure 3. At the top of the array, the veterans
system is shown both to modify the veteran's environment and to in-

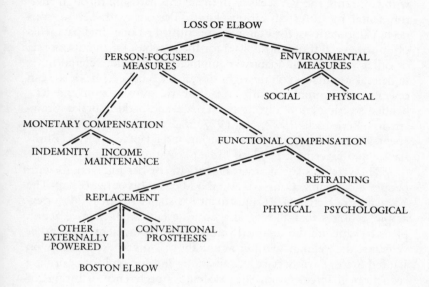

THE VETERAN'S COMPENSATORY ARRAY
Figure 3

tervene at a personal level. Recognizing that persons with upper-extremity amputations live in an environment designed for people with two arms, the VA seeks to mitigate this hardship through environmental measures of various kinds. Persons with service-connected amputations, for example, are entitled to one-time payments of up to several thousand dollars for the purchase of an automobile or other vehicle with adaptive equipment. When the veteran has a unilateral amputation on the right side, the VA believes he or she can operate an automobile with an automatic transmission and left-handed steering knob, directional signals, and parking brake (Stewart and Bernstock, 1977). In 1977, the Veterans Administration spent $28 million on modified housing and adapted vehicles (Burkhauser and Haveman, 1982, p. 114).

The veteran's social environment—his or her interactions with people and organizations—is also modified on his or her behalf. The Vietnam Era Veterans' Readjustment Assistance Act of 1974, for example, requires that all federal agencies establish affirmative action plans to expedite the disabled veteran's re-employment. Like other veterans, the veteran with an amputation is given extra points on United States Civil Service examinations and has seniority during a reduction in force. He or she also enjoys preference in hiring for many local and state government jobs. Section 402 of the Readjustment Assistance Act addresses discrimination in the private sector: employers with federal contracts of $10,000 or more not only may not discriminate against disabled veterans but must take affirmative action to employ and advance them (VA, 1982b).

The system through which a veteran obtains the benefits described in this chapter remains distinctly separate from other American social welfare systems. Beginning with the Eisenhower Commission in 1955, a series of formal inquiries have concluded that the American veteran should be mainstreamed—that is, that VA programs should be merged with civilian pensions, medical care, and so on (Obermann, 1965). The response to this proposition from most veterans groups, however, has been unambiguously and pointedly negative. Organizations like the American Legion, Disabled American Veterans (DAV), and Veterans of Foreign Wars have made it clear to elected officials that they favor a preferential as well as separate system of veterans benefits (Steiner, 1971; Rashkow, 1978). These groups contend that veterans should, by virtue of their contribution, receive from or through the federal government more and better services than other Americans. So far, those who would "normalize" veterans have been stymied in their attempts.

Veterans are also more likely than individuals in other systems to receive the benefits to which they are entitled. Unlike recipients of public assistance VA beneficiaries are not stigmatized (Steiner, 1971; Rashkow, 1978). On the contrary, they are generally thought to deserve whatever government can provide. Similarly, they are neither ignorant of nor intimidated by the agency whose mandate is to serve them. The Veterans Administration is highly visible and approaches its clientele sympathetically. A pensioner who receives income maintenance payments, for example, is asked to file only a simple annual income report. There is no investigation of his or her statement, and because the system operates at the national level, veterans are free to relocate without having to prove eligibility to a new state welfare bureaucracy (Steiner, 1971). Veterans organizations take pains to engage potential beneficiaries in the veterans system; outreach workers search out eligible persons who are not receiving benefits and aid them in enrolling in VA programs. Once a veteran has become a VA client, these groups offer advocacy services, in the clinic as described above or, for example, in the appeals process. Here veterans group personnel doggedly pursue resolution in the client's favor and often achieve reversal of unfavorable rulings (Steiner, 1971; interviews with VA and veterans group officials). Thus the veteran finds him or herself in a benefits system that is relatively generous and largely accessible. It is, so to speak, a barrier-free claims structure.

As Figure 3 indicates, the veterans system offers person-focused compensation in monetary and functional form. The veteran is entitled to cash benefits whether or not his or her disability is service-connected, although income support is provided on two tracks. On the first, the veteran whose amputation is service-connected receives "compensation," a monthly payment scaled to the amount of disability suffered for as long as he or she lives. He or she is given a percentage rating reflecting the severity of the impairment and a cash award that is considered compensatory for lost earning potential. Cash payments to veterans with service-connected amputations are set by law. They are the same for all individuals with the same disability rating and do not change with changes in employment status. "Compensation" is really a cross between indemnity and income maintenance: a fixed sum payable over an indeterminate period.

Veterans with service-connected amputations who have lost their dominant arm above the elbow are rated 90 percent disabled. As of October 1982, they received $729 per month in compensation (interviews with DAV officials; also VA, 1982a, n.p.). Almost two and a half million veterans received compensation payments in 1977 (Burkhauser and Haveman, 1982, p. 32). In September 1978, the VA was paying out approximately $1 billion annually to more than 700,000 persons suffering bone or joint losses or impairments, presumably including upper-extremity amputation (Rehab Group, Inc., 1979, p. 113).

On the second track of VA cash benefits, "pensions" are available to some persons with non-service-connected disabilities. Low-income veterans receive monthly checks if they are sixty-five years old or older, totally and permanently disabled, or an equivalent combination of the two—for example, if they are between fifty-five and sixty years old and 60 percent disabled (Rashkow, 1978, p. 57). The amount of the pension varies inversely with income, with a maximum annual payment of about $5,000 (VA, 1982b, n.p.). Housebound pensioners and those who require special care receive another monthly sum. In 1985 the total number of participants was about one million.

The importance of monetary compensation to the disabled veteran's configuration of benefits is evidenced by the size of the cash awards and by the activity of veterans groups in securing these benefits. The disability compensation and pension programs cost the VA approximately $7 billion a year in 1978 (Burkhauser and Haveman, 1982, p. 109). Many of those who receive these monies are members of politically active veterans groups that themselves seem to stress monetary benefits. Disabled American Veterans, the organization whose sole mandate is to represent veterans with service-connected disabilities, seems exemplary. In its 484 1982–83 resolutions

(DAV, 1983), DAV explicitly addressed compensatory technology only four times. The group lent its support to legislation that would make all telephones accessible to hearing-impaired persons (Resolution No. 069). DAV requested increased funds for housing adaptation and mortgage subsidies for adapted housing (Nos. 067 and 336). And it drew attention to a finding by the VA's Office of Program Evaluation that Prosthetics and Sensory Aids Service personnel had not been properly trained to execute management tasks; DAV resolved to press for legislation to provide funds for the recommended training (No. 369). Some number of the remaining resolutions concerned non-monetary benefits, and many of these were employment-related. But by far the majority of the DAV stands were taken on monetary compensation: who gets what at what rate for how long? One DAV service officer interviewed for this study confirmed the organization's emphasis on compensation payments. Service officers apparently spend relatively little time securing housing or medical benefits, for example. But they do pursue cash awards. In fact, they represent disabled veterans before Social Security Disability Insurance officials when SSDI payments are in jeopardy. At least in the Boston Office, DAV staff are more likely to aid disabled veterans in securing civilian monetary benefits than in garnering the non-cash benefits of the veterans system. A national DAV official described cash and medical (including rehabilitation) benefits as running "neck and neck" for the attention of the organization (interview).

In 1981, the head of a smaller veterans organization, Vietnam Veterans of America, was highly critical of the disability compensation program. Robert Muller is himself paraplegic and was receiving about $2,000 a month from the VA, but he contemned this compensatory mode: "You either survive or you do what most of the guys do, which is take your compensation check, which is ridiculously high. It's [expletive] blood money! . . . They have no purpose in life, no [expletive] meaning, no sense of self-worth or self-respect." Muller urged that the VA utilize its resources, not for cash payments, but to provide business opportunities for disabled veterans (Klein, 1981, p. 64). His objections to the existing program are ironic. Veterans disability compensation is independent of employment out of deference for the veteran. Unlike monetary benefits to other groups, veterans compensation is not designed to motivate the recipient's future labor force participation.

Functional compensation is another of the veteran's options, and it takes two forms (see Figure 3). The veteran with an amputation may be trained to function with one arm, or the amputated arm may be replaced with a device, like the VA Elbow, that carries out selected arm functions. As noted in Chapter 1, many routine tasks can be done with one hand, and if the client desires, the VA will teach him or her to function without a prosthesis. There is also a psychological aspect to this service. Therapists help clients adapt to living with one arm in a world of two-armed people (interviews with VA clinic staff).

Many potentially employable veterans with service-connected disabilities qualify for a vocational rehabilitation and training benefit. VA-sponsored vocational rehabilitation takes place in school and job settings and in 1982 could last as long as four full-time years or an equivalent mix of full- and part-time hours. The veteran may also receive a subsistence allowance for the duration of the training. In 1982, if he or she trained full time and had no dependents, the stipend, in addition to the disability compensation benefit, was $282 per month (VA, 1982b, p. 19). In 1976, the National Research Council found that the Veterans Administration was spending an average of $5,000 on a disabled veteran's vocational rehabilitation; the corresponding figure for the combined federal/state Vocational Rehabilitation Program was $800 (NRC, 1976, p. 22). Veterans with severe service-connected disabilities may receive training in independent living through the vocational rehabilitation program (Levitan and Taggart, 1977).

The Veteran and the Boston Elbow

Veterans with amputations enjoy a full array of compensatory options. Their physical environments can be modified and their oppor-

tunities for employment enhanced. They receive a fixed sum of
money if their amputations are service-connected, and they qualify
for a pension if their disabilities are not service-connected but their
income is low. Veterans with amputations receive physical, psychological, and vocational rehabilitation services (none of which presup-
pose a prosthesis). Their physicians will prescribe any prosthetic device, including the VA Elbow, that is medically appropriate and to
the veteran's liking.

Two aspects of this compensatory array deserve comment. First,
its offerings include both prosthetic arms and measures that minimize the need for these devices. No prosthesis can fully replace the
human arm; rehabilitation engineering can hope to reproduce only
some subset of arm functions and meanings. Thus a prosthesis is always less than adequate, and non-prosthetic strategies, like learning
to cook with one hand, are neither useless nor necessarily inferior to
wearing a prosthetic device. The same is true in a less obvious way of
measures like preference in federal hiring and disability compensation payments. These represent alternatives to physical restoration
when the latter is viewed as a means to financial independence. Of
course, veterans preference policies in no way preclude use of a prosthesis, but neither do they require it, and favorable hiring practices
have the potential to lessen the importance of limb replacement in
earning a living. Disability compensation is similar in this respect.
These cash benefits are sufficiently large that the veteran, who receives a fixed amount regardless of his or her income or assets, may
not need to maximize his or her employability by wearing a prosthesis. Monetary compensation is a particularly appealing alternative to
hardware and may even divert the veteran's attention from prosthetic
benefits. Cash, after all, has been proven effective, and is lighter and
less noisy than an artificial arm. Moreover, money benefits can always be used to purchase a device, whereas no prosthesis is trans-
mutable into cash. This is not to say that the veteran, however large
his or her compensation payment, is easily distracted from the loss of
an arm. On the contrary, the human arm is so remarkable and the
loss therefore so great that even the best prosthesis is a poor substitute. Under these conditions, alternatives to prosthetics may be
preferable.

Second, the Veterans Administration has fashioned its own elbow prosthesis, described above. The VA Elbow is less sophisticated technologically than a myoelectric arm, and one PSAS official interviewed for this study opined that the VA's device was almost useless (interview). But even if the VA Elbow is an inferior prosthesis, it competes with the Boston Elbow for use by veterans. Both are battery-powered elbow joints and differ significantly in this respect from the more common body-powered prostheses. Both require battery recharging and therefore the kind of user who can plan ahead. The VA Elbow is neither myoelectric nor proportional, but these differences are more subtle than the fact of external power— especially if the prosthesis is prescribed as a *benefit* rather than as the means to some functional end. The VA Elbow is a credible competitor for the Boston Elbow not only because it may be more accessible to VA clinic teams or a real functional alternative but because it adequately signifies that the veteran is receiving compensation of every kind. One long-time rehabilitation policy-maker concluded that the veterans system is a *benefits,* not a rehabilitation, system because disabled veterans are not required to work (interview with the former Rehabilitation Services Administration commissioner). According to an official in the VA's Department of Veterans Benefits, the word "rehabilitation" does not describe the transfer of resources to VA clients (interview). And the structure of the veteran's compensatory array itself bespeaks an emphasis on benefits over functioning. Options are independent, dispensed on the principle that the veteran with a service-connected disability deserves whatever benefits the system can muster.

The veteran's compensatory array, including the VA Elbow, has strong political and normative roots. Although it is beyond the scope of this study to disentangle the political power of veterans groups from the belief that veterans are deserving clients, it is clear that the influence of both is felt by those who administer veterans programs. Policy-makers and practitioners in many parts of the veterans system reported experiencing pressure from veterans organizations to resolve matters in the veteran's favor (interviews; also Klein, 1981; Bonafede, 1982); the groups maintain offices in Washington and in every VA hospital and regional office. When Ronald Reagan appointed as VA administrator a man who described his clients as wanting "more, more, more," for example, this appointee's tenure was brief, terminated by political pressure from veterans organizations (Bonafede, 1982, p. 1716). Similarly, Congress rejected half of the first set of Reagan's cuts in the VA budget, and some of the cuts that were made were quickly restored. The political power of veterans derives at least in part from their numbers. Five million belong to veterans organizations, and veterans and their 60 million survivors and dependents constitute about 40 percent of the population of the United States (Bonafede, 1982, p. 1715).

The veterans system operates on norms as well as power. It would be hard to overstate the consistency with which VA staff interviewed for this study expressed commitment to the veteran with an amputation and to other veterans. A Prosthetics Representative quoted the Veterans Administration motto, from Lincoln's second inaugural address, in describing his client as "he who shall have borne the battle" (interview). A VA prosthetist explained that his job was to provide "the best prosthesis possible" to every eligible veteran, whether the disability was service-connected or not. He indicated his assent when the Prosthetics Representative added that "cost is secondary to need" (joint interview). A VA orthopedist portrayed the agency's approach to prosthetics as assuming that a veteran with a service-connected disability "merits anything we can give him" and that veterans should have the opportunity to use any device or combination of devices that might mitigate their loss. When I asked about comparable care for Medicaid patients, he reminded me, "You and I are putting out that dollar"—it has not been earned through military service (interview).

The veterans system is not a monolith. In addition to its comprising three kinds of organizations—the VA, congressional committees, and veterans groups—the system serves three sub-populations—able-bodied veterans, veterans with service-connected disabilities, and veterans with non-service-connected disabilities. Both groups of disabled veterans receive benefits, but service-connected disability is more generously compensated. There is a two-tiered norm. The American Legion casts veterans' non-service-connected pensions as delayed compensation for military services rendered, an unavoidable cost of war that should be paid gladly. This definition of the issue diverts the public's gaze from the non-service-connected cause of the veteran's disability to a resultant neediness that seems unjustifiable in light of his contribution (Steiner, 1971). But Disabled American Veterans makes it clear that they serve only veterans with service-connected disabilities. The national DAV takes the position that, although in principle they have no objection to benefits for other veterans, the organization will oppose any program that jeopardizes the gains of its own constituency (interview with national DAV officer). One DAV official stated that he approved of veterans pensions because disabled veterans should receive a larger benefit than disabled welfare recipients do, but he and others in the veterans system distinguished between the overwhelming worthiness of the veteran with a service-connected disability and the weaker claim of his non-service-connected counterpart (interview).

It is the veteran/non-veteran split that is most pronounced even among disabled people. The head of a national disability rights organization finds veterans difficult to enlist in collective action in spite of the fact that they know their rights as people with disabilities. He has concluded that disabled veterans are secure in the knowledge that the Veterans Administration will provide for them (interview). He might have added that veterans groups are reluctant to coalesce with people less politically powerful than themselves.

The delayed diffusion of the Boston Elbow through the veterans system results, at least in part, from the number and range of compensatory options that that system provides. Government offers the veteran every strategy for coping with functional loss. This array, which derives from political power and shared norms regarding military service, both lessens the need to learn about the Boston Elbow and makes its use less appealing to those who learn about it. The specific mechanism that slows diffusion of a compensatory technology such as the Boston Elbow has not been named here. It is difficult to observe. But innovation researchers cite "market pull" as the primary force in diffusion of any technology (Utterback, 1974), and it is plausible that in a system with so many compensatory options, the veteran and his agents did not exert the requisite "pull" on the Boston Elbow. Ironically, the veterans system may distribute *too many* compensatory options to make diffusion of the Boston Elbow an object of its attention.

The dominant diffusion models are inadequate to reveal this irony. They fail to account for the many alternatives to the Boston Elbow and for the commitment of government to the veteran. These are issues distinct from the Elbow's lifecycle and communications about the device. In the view presented here, diffusion is shaped by compensatory alternatives and political alliances that fall outside the kinds of progress technologies are said to make. This theme will recur: that government diffuses particular technologies in a context of competing measures and political relationships.

3
Holding Down a Job
The Worker

American workers sometimes suffer the loss of an arm. When they do, government may offer any of three sets of compensatory options: workers' compensation insurance, Social Security Disability Insurance (SSDI), and the federal/state Vocational Rehabilitation (VR) Program. Workers may qualify for one or more of these programs; eligibility is defined by past, present, and potential participation in the labor force. Specifically, workers' compensation insurance covers workers injured in the workplace, SSDI compensates the worker disabled anywhere, and the VR Program serves disabled individuals who appear to have the potential for work.

This chapter will chart the compensatory options of the worker with an amputation. Each of the arrays presented corresponds to a single program—that may or may not offer the Boston Elbow. Workers' compensation insurance and the Vocational Rehabilitation Program operate to put the disabled person to work. To the extent that the Boston Elbow serves this purpose, one would expect the device to be a benefit. Similarly, workers who are eligible for SSDI also receive Medicare benefits, and one would expect a health insurance program for disabled workers to offer a rehabilitation technology like the Boston Elbow. In fact, none of the programs depicted in this chapter consistently features the Boston Elbow. This is true despite the fact that it originated in a workers' compensation insurance company for the purpose of returning disabled workers to work.

Government faces countervailing forces in diffusing the Boston

Elbow to the worker with an amputation. First, workers' compensation insurance is in most states purchased in the private sector, where the Boston Elbow serves to differentiate one firm's product. Second, SSDI, a health insurance program for former workers, is responsible only for what is "medically necessary," and this only after a two-year waiting period. Third, the VR Program has an expanded mandate that both encourages attention to persons with amputations and strains the resources available for compensatory technology. The worker is more likely than the veteran and citizen to have a Boston Elbow, but he or she is less likely to have one than might be expected.

The Worker's Compensatory Options: Workers' Compensation

Workers' compensation is an insurance program that covers workers in virtually all firms. It provides benefits to employees who are injured or contract a disease on the job. Federal law requires workers' compensation coverage, but it is essentially a state program. The scope of its benefits varies from state to state, and in some jurisdictions, employers pay directly into a state workers' compensation fund. In others, including Massachusetts, private insurance companies write policies and handle claims against employers. In 1978, $5.8 billion in cash benefits were paid out nationally to over a million injured or ill workers through the workers' compensation program. Over 90 percent of American wage and salary employees were covered, at a cost to employers of $17 billion, including benefits, operating expenses, and litigation (Price, 1980, p. 6; Burkhauser and Haveman, 1982, p. 31).

The workers' compensation program assumes that workplace injury can result in functional loss and that this loss is compensable in various ways. Physicians use American Medical Association guidelines to evaluate a worker's injury and judge the extent of his or her impairment. Temporary and permanent, partial and total disabilities are usually specified. When an injured worker and the employer's insurer disagree about the worker's disability, either may bring the matter before a public body for resolution. In 1981, between 45,000 and 50,000 workers' compensation cases a year were handled without incident by insurance companies in Massachusetts. In another 12,000 to 15,000 cases, problems arise, and the state's Industrial Accidents Board (IAB) reviews the specifics of each injury to answer the following questions: was the worker in fact injured or made ill in the workplace? What is the extent of his or her impairment? Is the worker able now to return to work (interview with IAB commissioner)?

When above-elbow amputation is the subject of an IAB review, the first question is generally not difficult to answer. Heart conditions and some kinds of cancer resist attribution to a single cause, but the reasons for loss of an arm are usually apparent. The second question, too, is readily answered: loss of a limb is unambiguously serious. The answer to the third question, however, is less obvious, and several disagreements on this point have come before the Massachusetts IAB in the last decade (interview with IAB commissioner). Disputes usually originate with claims by workers' compensation insurers that beneficiaries are capable of working and are therefore ineligible for continued support. Beneficiaries in turn contend that they remain too disabled to return to work. Resolution may hinge on an offer of rehabilitation services. On the basis of a worker's age, educational background, and disability, the Board may instruct the insurer to rehabilitate the worker further, to the point where employability is no longer a question. Replacing a lost arm with a sophisticated prosthesis hastens rehabilitation and is likely to be perceived this way by members of the IAB. In fact, providing a Boston Elbow may itself constitute sufficient rehabilitation to justify termination of workers' compensation benefits (interview with IAB commisioner).

The Workers' Compensation Array

At the top of the array (see Figure 4), workers' compensation insurance provides both environmental modification and measures focused on the person, although the former is a relatively minor aspect of the program. According to a member of the Massachusetts

72

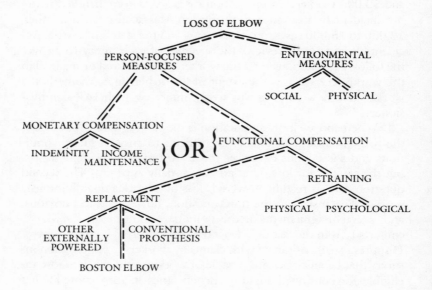

THE WORKER'S COMPENSATORY ARRAY:
WORKERS' COMPENSATION
Figure 4

Industrial Accident Board, the IAB sometimes suggests home or workplace modification. Unlike other benefits, however, environmental adaptation is entirely the prerogative of the insurer (interview with IAB commissioner). Officials at the Liberty Mutual Insurance Company distinguished further between automobile and home adaptation, on the one hand, and measures taken in the workplace, on the other. The latter are provided only at the discretion of the employer, who decides independently whether or how to reinstate the disabled employee. When an insurer does undertake environmental modification, it is always for the purpose of returning the worker to work. Automobile adaptation is a good example (interviews with IAB and Liberty Mutual officials).

The workers' compensation program intervenes primarily at the personal level, where it provides monetary and functional responses to disability. In Massachusetts, cash benefits take two forms. First, the disabled worker receives compensation for his or her specific anatomical loss, which itself is considered in two parts, functional loss and disfigurement. In 1983, functional loss of an amputated dominant arm meant a fixed payment, or indemnity, of $9,000. The fixed sum for loss of the minor arm was $8,000, and the maximum disfigurement benefit for an above-elbow amputation was $6,600. Thus the workers' compensation beneficiary who had lost most of his dominant arm received a fixed amount of almost $16,000. Neither wearing an above-elbow prosthesis (like the Boston Elbow) nor returning to work bears on the size of this one-time award (interview with IAB commissioner). The award can of course be used to purchase a Boston Elbow.

The second form of workers' compensation cash benefits is weekly income maintenance payments, either temporary or permanent. The amount received is generally a percentage of the recipient's former wage, up to some maximum. In Massachusetts, the benefit for temporary total disability is two-thirds of the worker's average weekly wage or about $300, whichever is less. Temporary partial disability is said to exist when the injured or ill worker is capable of work but at a lower wage than he or she was receiving when he or she became disabled. The benefit is the difference between the old and new wage, and payments are made for a total of 250 weeks. At the end of this period, a worker must qualify for permanent total disability benefits or lose the award. Permanent benefits are set at a recipient's temporary total disability rate and are paid as long as the disabling condition is manifest (interviews at IAB and Liberty Mutual).

Richard V. Burkhauser and Robert H. Haveman have calculated the 1978 annual benefits accruing to three hypothetical workers' compensation beneficiaries each of whom is totally permanently disabled and has a non-working spouse and two children. The worker who has earned half the average annual income over his or her employment lifetime receives $4,586 per year in Washington, D.C. (a generous jurisdiction) and $3,051 in Oklahoma (a less generous one). His or her net replacement rate is 62 percent. To a worker who earned the average annual income during his or her employment life, Washington pays $6,115 and Oklahoma $3,900, with a net income replacement rate of 43 percent. An individual who has earned twice the average annual income over his or her lifetime of employment receives $12,229 in Washington but only $3,900 again in Oklahoma (Burkhauser and Haveman, 1982, p. 58). The National Commission of State Workmen's Compensation Laws recommended in the early 1970s that the maximum weekly payment for temporary total disability be greater than or equal to 133.3 percent of the worker's average weekly wage. The Commission set a July 1977 target date; as of 1978, only seven jurisdictions provided benefits on this scale, and nine sites, including Massachusetts, limited workers' compensation payments to two-thirds of the average weekly wage (Price, 1980, p. 7).

The workers' compensation insurer seeks to minimize amounts paid to claimants. The fixed-sum portion of workers' compensation benefits does not change with the claimant's work status, but the income-maintenance portion is terminated or reduced when he or she returns to work. It is to the advantage of the insurer, therefore, to expedite the worker's re-employment. Workers' compensation insurance clients—that is, employers who purchase policies—also benefit from a worker's return to work. A firm's premium is experience-rated; it is increased or decreased depending on the costs incurred by injured employees. Re-employment, by capping income-maintenance payments, also acts to minimize premiums.

Figure 4 indicates that functional compensation is another of the workers' compensation program's offerings. Some form of retraining is included in most states, and these services are generally bought by workers' compensation insurers from independent facilities. A number of firms have appended pre-existing rehabilitation centers, but the Liberty Mutual Insurance Company is unique in having had its own rehabilitation facility for over forty years. Liberty Mutual decided to enter the rehabilitation field after a study of the firm's workers' compensation beneficiaries revealed that few of them were using rehabilitation technologies or had returned to work. When at the end of World War II rehabilitation became a national priority, Liberty Mutual found a model in the Veterans Administration and planned to open more than a single center. But by the end of the 1950s, hospital-based centers began to appear, and Liberty Mutual was able to send rehabilitation clients through satisfactory public or private facilities in their communities (interview with Liberty Mutual Rehabilitation Center official).

The Liberty Mutual Rehabilitation Center is located in Boston. It is part of a larger medical services center and is linked with the Liberty Mutual Research Center, which has the capacity to fabricate artificial limbs. The rehabilitation facility serves beneficiaries in the Boston area and those from other geographic areas who need services not available to them locally. Especially difficult cases, for example where multiple injuries have been sustained, are frequently referred to the Boston Center. Approximately eighty cases are served there at any one time, typically men in their late thirties with hand or back injuries who spend thirty-plus days at the Rehabilitation Center (interview with Rehabilitation Center official).

A common offering of the workers' compensation array is replacement—the provision of prosthetic devices. Generally the worker's physician chooses the appropriate prosthesis, but the state in which an injury occurs also influences the replacement decision. Workers' compensation legislation varies substantially from state to state. In some, injured workers are entitled to a one-time prosthetic benefit only. In other states, like Massachusetts, prosthetic services are provided for the rest of a worker's life. Not only must an insurer replace a worn prosthesis, but the worker's changing anatomical and occupational needs must be met with new devices. State workers' compensation policy bears also on the initial fitting of an artificial limb. One prosthetist explained that he hesitates to fit someone from a one-prosthesis state with a sophisticated elbow whose service life may be as short as five years. Similarly, a Boston Elbow is more likely than a mechanical arm to require expert repair and may be inappropriate for a person who does not have a back-up device and access to an expert. These distinctions find poignant expression among workers with amputations who come to the Liberty Mutual Rehabilitation Center from various states; two individuals with the same injury, and perhaps even the same employer, retire to their hotels at night with two different arms (interview with Liberty Mutual official).

The Boston Elbow appears as one compensatory option in the workers' compensation array. The device is distributed primarily by Liberty Mutual to its clients' workplace-injured employees, and the Elbow represents the company's efforts to provide extraordinary rehabilitation services. Liberty Mutual is the largest writer of workers' compensation policies in the world and the fourth largest American company in the property-casualty field. In fiscal year 1981, the firm's assets stood at more than $7.5 billion, with $2.8 billion in premiums, approximately 40 percent of which was for workers' compensation coverage (Liberty Mutual Insurance Company, 1984, pp. 3, 20).

In addition to being an insurance company, Liberty Mutual manufactures the Boston Elbow. The company holds the patent to the Russell-Ohlenbusch version of the device and fabricates it in a small shop in Hopkinton. Basic mechanical and electronic components are purchased locally, and Liberty Mutual assembles the arm and readies it for the user. The shop also repairs malfunctioning Elbows that are returned by users or prosthetists (interview with Liberty Mutual engineer). Liberty Mutual pursues two strategies in marketing the Boston Elbow: to exhibit at professional meetings, mostly of physicians, and draw media attention to the prosthesis; and to offer two-day training courses in the Boston Elbow to rehabilitation teams of doctors, prosthetists, and occupational therapists from other facilities. Liberty Mutual hopes to interest practitioners outside the workers' compensation system in the device (interview with Liberty Mutual official).

Workers' Compensation and the Boston Elbow

The Boston Elbow is one way in which Liberty Mutual puts workers with amputations back to work; to the extent that the Elbow's performance surpasses that of other prostheses, it is more likely to facilitate re-employment. It has not been possible to determine exactly how many workers' compensation beneficiaries wear a Boston Elbow, still less the number for whom the prosthesis is critical, but of nine Liberty Mutual rehabilitants contacted by phone or mail, five reported that the Boston Elbow was "very important" to their jobs. One professional and long-term participant in the Boston Elbow project conjectured that the prosthesis has not made a difference in Liberty Mutual's income-maintenance payments. His informal assessment was that the firm could have paid lifetime benefits to all Boston Elbow wearers for as much as the development of the device has cost the firm so far (interview). But Liberty Mutual has built a valuable reputation for rehabilitation-mindedness with undertakings like the Boston Elbow. In fact, every company official interviewed indicated that the Elbow is an important means of (insurance) product differentiation. The device not only attracts clients, but it appeals to employers who are themselves concerned about rehabilitation—responsible employers who may have fewer workplace accidents. Despite the fact that workers' compensation premiums reflect a client's safety record, the insurer's losses are not entirely recoverable (interviews). Insurance companies therefore compete for the least accident-prone firms.

Comparison of the Boston Elbow and the Utah Arm (see Table 1) suggests a direct effect of public policy on prosthetic design. The two prostheses derive from the same idea; as a result, both are myoelectric and proportional. They differ in several ways, however, and these differences seem to indicate a divergence of objectives. First, the Utah Arm is a more attractive prosthesis than the Boston Elbow. It has a slimmer forearm and is less noisy, and because it has complete free swing, it is also more natural looking. The Boston Elbow, in contrast, has a boxy forearm and only a thirty-degree free swing. It weighs more and moves more slowly than the Utah Arm but will also lift more weight. The makers of the Boston Elbow favor a capacity for simultaneous movement of the elbow and the ter-

minal device, this having been Glimcher's concern in initiating the
Boston Elbow project. When worn with a cable-operated terminal
device, both the Elbow and the Arm pass the "Glimcher test," but
when the Utah Arm is worn with a powered terminal device, the two
degrees of freedom almost always have a single control site and
therefore can be operated only sequentially. Technically, both the
Utah Arm and the Boston Elbow can be wired either for simultaneous movement of elbow and terminal device or for single-site control. Liberty Mutual has chosen to implement the first, and Motion
Control, maker of the Utah Arm, the second option. Another difference is that the Boston Elbow runs for about eight hours and then
requires two hours of recharging, during which it cannot be worn.
The Utah Arm runs for about the same amount of time (half as long
if a powered terminal device is being worn), but the battery pack can
be removed for recharging and replaced on the spot with batteries
that are fully charged. This means that, although recharging the
Utah Arm takes sixteen hours to the Boston Elbow's two, with a sufficient number of batteries and chargers, users of the Utah Arm can
have a functioning prosthesis whenever they wish.

The Boston Elbow emerges from this discussion as a "worker's"
arm. If it is to be worn primarily at work, cosmetic strengths may be
less important than functional ones, and eight hours of power may
suffice. A brochure for the Boston Elbow features a photograph of a
middle-aged man in a tie repairing a television set. The caption
reads: "Soldering requires the precise positioning of both the solder
and the iron." Later in the same advertisement, the Boston Elbow's
battery is described as powering "a full 8-hour workday." One VA
official referred to the device as a "clunker," an arm for a "working
man" (interview), and in correspondence for this study, a Liberty
Mutual official identified Boston Elbow wearers by occupation as
well as name and address. One retired user reported that his Elbow
needed adjustment but that he would not return to Liberty Mutual
for repairs because other, younger people deserved the firm's full attention (personal communication). Liberty Mutual in turn indicated
that the firm's interest in making repairs for this individual was diminished because he no longer needed the prosthesis for work (interview). This work orientation is not implicit in above-elbow pros-

thetics. In a limited number of interviews, Motion Control officials spoke consistently about reproducing all of the human arm, about building a device that *feels* real to the user, and the Utah Arm brochure features a young woman in blue jeans socializing with other young people. But the lens through which Liberty Mutual views its prosthesis is work—not a surprising bias given the firm's interest in the workers' compensation insurance market and the fact that the Boston Elbow's development and refinement took place among workers' compensation beneficiaries—individuals who had been injured in the workplace, and whose re-employment was at the heart of the rehabilitation process.

Ironically, it is the value of the Boston Elbow to the Liberty Mutual Insurance Company that may be frustrating diffusion of the device. According to Liberty Mutual's 1980 annual report, there is "vicious competition" in the insurance market generally, while in the workers' compensation market, competition has "reached a feverish pitch" (Liberty Mutual Insurance Company, 1981, pp. 2, 3). The Boston Elbow is a means of product differentiation as well as an aid to rehabilitation. Surely it is particularly valuable in a competitive workers' compensation insurance market, and the firm may hesitate to diffuse the device to other workers' compensation insurers. According to one Liberty Mutual official, an occasional "courtesy" is extended to competing firms. A worker whose injury precludes use of other prosthetic devices may come to Liberty Mutual to be fitted with a Boston Elbow. But this arrangement is "touchy," evocative of the firm's mixed motives: to rehabilitate workers and to protect its interests (interview). Another official denied that diffusion to competing firms is problematic. He explained that it is simply inefficient to market to insurers, that he concentrates on diffusion to rehabilitation professionals because they are most likely to prescribe or suggest the device (interview). This is true enough, but rehabilitation professionals do not pay for prostheses. Other insurers do, especially when a worker's arm promises to reduce expenditures, and these firms would therefore seem a reasonable target for diffusion activities. Of course, other insurers have to be willing to buy the Boston Elbow. In interviews conducted for this study, officials of two major insurance companies expressed competitiveness with Liberty Mutual and skepticism about the firm's reputation for superior rehabilitation services.

The workers' compensation beneficiary, in summary, may or may not receive a Boston Elbow. The array depicted above is one of intervention primarily at the individual level. Benefits virtually always include payment for anatomical loss and monetary compensation for functional loss until the worker returns to work. Functional compensation, including the fitting of a prosthesis, is also provided, but when functionality is achieved, the beneficiary must relinquish the income-maintenance portion of his or her cash payment. To the extent that the Boston Elbow restores lost functioning, it is well-suited to workers' compensation insurers. But in those states where the program enlists private insurers, firms will compete for the best rehabilitation record. This may keep Liberty Mutual from diffusing the Elbow through other insurers and other insurers from buying Liberty Mutual's device.

The Worker's Compensatory Options: Social Security Disability Insurance

Social Security Disability Insurance is a program of benefits covering any American worker who has contributed to the Social Security system in at least half of the forty quarters preceding his or her claim. SSDI applies to disability of any origin, not only to disability resulting from injury or illness in the workplace. It is thus broader in its coverage than workers' compensation insurance, although unlike the latter, SSDI requires the worker to have paid into the system. In 1981, almost 2.8 million disabled workers received an average monthly SSDI payment of $413 (Lando et al., 1982, p. 3). SSDI is funded through payroll taxes.

A worker covered by Social Security Disability Insurance receives benefits if several conditions are met. He or she must suffer a medically certifiable disability that is expected to last at least twelve months or result in death. This disability must prevent him or her from participating in "substantial gainful activity" (SGA) and must already have done so during the five months immediately preceding certification for the SSDI program. For SSDI, disability is a dichotomous variable: a worker is either disabled or not. The determination process, however, includes assessment of the potential beneficiary's vocational characteristics as well as his or her health status. A disabled individual who is by medical criteria incapable of doing the type of work he or she has done, and capable, by the same criteria, of doing a type of work he or she is certain not to find is still considered to be incapable of "substantial gainful activity." This "vocational standard" was formalized in 1978, but it was probably exercised in a discretionary way from the start of the program (Burkhauser and Haveman, 1982, p. 42). Determining SSDI eligibility is a responsibility of state vocational rehabilitation agencies, who receive federal funding for this activity. In fiscal year 1982, the Massachusetts Rehabilitation Commission (MRC) made determinations in 54,000 new SSDI and SSI (Supplemental Security Income) cases and reviewed the status of another 11,000 enrollees in these programs (MRC, 1983, p. 28).

Social Security Disability Insurance is explicitly a program for workers, including workers with amputations. According to the Social Security Administration (SSA), SSDI provides benefits to "insured workers," "workers with long-term disabilities that interfere with their ability to work." Indeed disability itself is defined for the program as the "inability to engage in any substantial gainful activity" (cited in Smith and Lilienfeld, 1972, p. 1). SSA's emphasis on the client's employment history and employability not only expresses the mandate of SSDI but distinguishes this program from government activity on the "welfare" model. A history of work is regarded as evidence of a beneficiary's worthiness. It is a "revelatory sign," proof to program officials that the client is the kind of person who deserves their support in a time of need (Stone, 1984, p. 101).

The Social Security Disability Insurance Array
As noted in Figure 5, SSDI intervenes only at the personal level and offers both monetary and functional compensation. Burkhauser

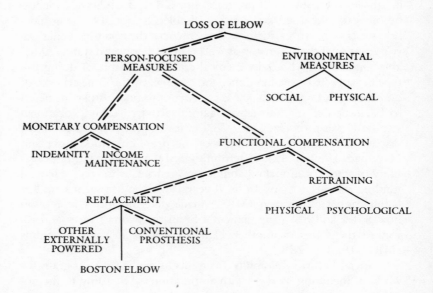

LOSS OF ELBOW

PERSON-FOCUSED MEASURES

ENVIRONMENTAL MEASURES

SOCIAL   PHYSICAL

MONETARY COMPENSATION

INDEMNITY   INCOME MAINTENANCE

FUNCTIONAL COMPENSATION

RETRAINING

REPLACEMENT

PHYSICAL   PSYCHOLOGICAL

OTHER EXTERNALLY POWERED   CONVENTIONAL PROSTHESIS

BOSTON ELBOW

——— Possible responses

— — — Actually provided

THE WORKER'S COMPENSATORY ARRAY:
SSDI
Figure 5

and Haveman have calculated 1978 SSDI benefits for three hypothetical workers with non-working spouses and two children each.
The worker who earned half the average income per year over his or
her working lifetime received $2,904, at a net income replacement
rate of 59 percent. The worker whose earnings were average was
paid $4,470 in SSDI benefits; his or her net income replacement rate
was 49 percent. And the most affluent worker, having earned twice
the average annual income, received $5,937, at a net income replace-
ment rate of 35 percent (Burkhauser and Haveman, 1982, p. 58).

Until 1980, Social Security Disability Insurance limited the
outside earnings of beneficiaries to $300 a month for nine
months—a "trial work period." At the end of this period, the SSDI
recipient entered a final three months of money benefits and then
was terminated from the program. The 1980 Social Security
Amendments responded to charges that the brevity of this final stage
was a disincentive to trial work, and the new law allows enrollees to
retain their disabled status (but not their cash benefits) for an additional year. During this time it is relatively easy for former beneficiaries to re-enroll in SSDI should their employment opportunities
turn out to be short-lived (OTA, 1982).

SSDI cash benefits have evolved since 1954, when the program
was initiated. In its earliest form, SSDI was a "disability freeze"—
that is, it was a way for workers to maintain their retirement benefits
during a period of disability. Benefits were not paid to the disabled
worker, but neither were they lost. SSDI functioned as a waiver to
premium. In 1956, an amendment established disability benefits
based on what the SSDI beneficiary would have received at retirement. The amended program was essentially an early retirement
plan, and recipients had to be at least fifty years of age to qualify
(Nagi, 1969; Howards et al., 1980). From 1958 on, SSDI eligibility
requirements were liberalized in several respects. For example, 1960
saw elimination of the age requirements and introduction of the trial
work period. The most significant change in SSDI was enacted in
1965: permanent total disability was replaced in the scheme of the
program with total disability for at least twelve months or resulting
in death. Thus, less seriously disabled workers began receiving
SSDI, workers who might after twelve months of benefits return to

work (Nagi, 1969; Howards et al., 1980). Originally a way to retire, SSDI had become for many a temporary measure.

SSDI provides functional compensation to workers with amputations through two programs, both of which offer retraining and replacement. The first is the federal/state Vocational Rehabilitation Program (the topic of the next section of this chapter). Eligibility for SSDI is determined by VR personnel (who are paid with Social Security funds), and eligible workers exhibiting a potential for reemployment are automatically referred for VR services; a prosthesis might be one such service. SSDI recipients have not been rehabilitated—that is, returned to SGA—in great numbers. The Massachusetts Rehabilitation Commission reports that in fiscal year 1981, out of a total of 3,245 SSDI clients served, fewer than 500 were rehabilitated. The number of rehabilitated SSDI clients actually fell between 1979 and 1981, this despite, or perhaps because of, an increase in the number of recipients served (MRC, 1982, p. 13). At the national level, researchers found that in fiscal year 1975, Vocational Rehabilitation accounted for $1.39 to $2.72 in savings to the SSDI trust fund per dollar spent to purchase services from the VR Program. SSDI costs would at this rate have been recovered in ten years. Unfortunately, rehabilitated beneficiaries returned to the SSDI rolls often enough that the expected payback from payroll taxes never materialized (McManus, 1981, cited in OTA, 1982, pp. 106–7). Explanations of this poor showing often cite economic disincentives to work inherent in the SSDI program—for example, the complete loss of benefits if employment terminates after at least one year (OTA, 1982, pp. 105–6). General unemployment may also contribute to lower labor force participation by SSDI clients. And because they must be totally disabled, even those recipients who show work potential must recover to a considerable degree. Finally, the federal government ceased, in fiscal year 1982, to provide funds specifically for the rehabilitation of SSDI and SSI recipients. MRC lost over $2.5 million it received from the federal SSDI and SSI programs in fiscal year 1981. The figure had been $4 million in fiscal year 1980 (MRC, 1983, p. 7).

The second program offering retraining and replacement to recipients of SSDI is Medicare. Since 1974, some individuals receiving SSDI benefits have also been eligible for health care under this program. The 1972 amendments to the Social Security Act provide for Medicare benefits to those disabled persons who have been enrolled in the SSDI program for twenty-four months. They are then entitled to all Medicare-reimbursable services and, like other Medicare beneficiaries, are required to contribute 20 percent of the cost of prosthetic devices and physical therapy.

The Medicare program offers automatic coverage of most inpatient services (Part A) and optional coverage of 80 percent of the cost of most out-patient services (Part B). In order to qualify for Medicare reimbursement, a prosthetic device must be "medically necessary." This requirement has three aspects. First, the device must be a *medical* technology, one that provides functional replacement of a human organ or limb lost through disease or trauma. Second, a prosthetic technology must be *necessary* and not solely desirable. The most basic replacement strategy will suffice. Third, a device must be medically necessary in the *specific case* for which it is being prescribed; reimbursement policy addresses not just the artifact but the context as well. An additional consideration in the reimbursement process is cost. The Medicare program will pay providers of devices only what program officials deem a "reasonable cost" (interview with former and present Medicare officials).

Does the Boston Elbow constitute a medically necessary technology under the Medicare program? It is impossible to say with certainty. Medicare reimbursement policy is formulated on a post-claim basis. That is, an individual medical technology is evaluated for coverage only after a provider or beneficiary has filed a claim for it (interview with Health Care Financing Administration [HCFA] officials; HCFA is the federal agency responsible for the Medicare program). According to staff at Massachusetts Blue Shield, the state's carrier for Medicare Part B, no claim for the Boston Elbow has ever been submitted (interview). If a claim were filed, Blue Shield would assemble a physician advisory panel. Its members would draw on the medical literature and their own expertise to determine if the Boston Elbow were appropriate to the case in question and if there were a less costly or already covered alternative to the device. When a technological innovation affects large numbers of Medicare beneficiaries, policy-makers at the federal level are more likely to consider a case themselves. The central office also makes

HCFA reimbursement policy vis-à-vis a technology *per se*. Carriers then derive the implication of these rulings for a particular case (interviews with Medicare officials).

Provider groups have a strong interest in Medicare policy-making. Not only does Medicare coverage confer consumer status on the program's beneficiaries, but Medicare policy is reputed to be a standard for private health insurance policies as well (interviews with HCFA officials and for-profit insurers). In the case of the Boston Elbow, negotiations in the early 1980s between HCFA and the American Orthotics and Prosthetics Association may have moved the device toward reimbursement. AOPA has worked with HCFA to elaborate Medicare's common procedures codes for prosthetics and orthotics, and myoelectric elbow prostheses do appear among the procedures included in the 1985 codification (interviews with HCFA and AOPA officials). But the relationship of coding to reimbursement is subtle. Naming a device does not mean that it constitutes a reimbursable cost, only that the question of reimbursement has been raised. According to HCFA, AOPA's goal has been to negotiate an increase in the "reasonable costs" of prosthetics and orthotics by differentiating the more sophisticated procedures (interview). Still, even an explicit Boston Elbow code might not be approved for payment. There would still be the matter of its medical necessity beyond what less expensive elbow prostheses can provide.

As noted above, Medicare benefits are extended to people with disabilities only after they have been SSDI recipients for twenty-four months. SSDI beneficiaries are by definition workers and may have private medical insurance and personal savings to fall back on when they are first disabled. In the case of the Boston Elbow, however, the two-year Medicare lag may be an obstacle to diffusion. It is the belief of many of the professionals interviewed for this study that the period immediately following amputation is best for prosthetic fittings. Immediate fitting not only has a strong restorative effect on the user, but makes the prosthesis a part of his or her body image. People with amputations generally settle on a compensatory strategy quickly; they sometimes decide before a prosthesis can be fitted that they function adequately with one arm. The new Medicare beneficiary has lived with an amputation for over two years. He or she is likely to have adapted to life without a prosthesis—or with one that was immediately affordable. On the other hand, prostheses do need to be replaced, and the person with an above-elbow amputation may submit a Medicare claim for a Boston Elbow to replace his or her current device.

Social Security Disability Insurance and the Boston Elbow

The Boston Elbow is not indigenous to SSDI the way it is to workers' compensation insurance. The device is at most a Medicare benefit for persons who have been receiving SSDI cash benefits for twenty-four months. And the Medicare beneficiary must pay 20 percent of the cost of any Elbow provided.

SSDI does not embrace the Boston Elbow for conceptual and political reasons. First, Social Security Disability Insurance does not operate on the principle of liability. It insures the worker, rather than his or her employer or other party to his or her disability. The impetus for SSDI benefits, therefore, is not to undo what has been done to the worker so much as to help him or her cope with the aftermath. The limb *per se* is less important to SSDI, as may be inferred from the program's choice of income maintenance over indemnity.

Another factor bearing on the provision of a Boston Elbow is that, although the federal government stands to gain from returning SSDI beneficiaries to the workforce, the SSDI program is not itself responsible for this outcome. Rather the federal/state Vocational Rehabilitation Program is charged with putting SSDI beneficiaries back to work, and VR monies may be spent for technologies that will facilitate employment. SSDI recipients who are not also VR clients may obtain a Boston Elbow only through Medicare—an explicitly medical, as opposed to vocational, program and one whose clients are mostly above retirement age. Assuming the Boston Elbow is especially well suited to the workplace, it is unlikely to find its way into the SSDI program.

SSDI does not compete with other insurers for clients. As part of the Social Security system, the program is well established, and participation is mandatory. SSDI is in fact a reluctant benefactor. National old-age insurance did not originally include coverage for disability, which was acknowledged to be a knottier social problem than old age, or at least to be more difficult to define (Stone, 1984).

Now policy-makers are trying to shorten SSDI rolls, which grew especially quickly after the liberalization of eligibility requirements in 1965. Between 1966 and 1976, the number of SSDI recipients (including dependents) rose 230 percent and the amount of benefits 450 percent to $8.4 billion. The program paid benefits to almost 2.9 million disabled workers at its peak in 1978 (Lando et al., 1982, p. 3). The number of SSDI beneficiaries then began to fall, and 1980 legislation accelerated this decline with more frequent case review. In 1981, the Reagan administration set out to trim $3.4 billion from the cost of the program, and by 1982, 139,000 recipients had been dropped from the rolls (Cater, 1982, p. 1512). (Two-thirds of those who appealed termination were reinstated by Social Security administrative law judges [Cater, 1982, p. 1512].) Unlike Liberty Mutual, which faces considerable competition in the insurance market, SSDI does not need to lure clients with the real or symbolic benefits of the Boston Elbow.

In summary, the Boston Elbow may diffuse through SSDI, but there are reasons to believe it will not. The SSDI beneficiary is entitled to income maintenance that will cease when he or she returns to work, but SSDI does not bear direct responsibility for his or her reemployment, and Medicare attends to medical necessity alone. SSDI has little incentive for offering the Elbow. The twenty-four-month Medicare lag encourages beneficiaries to find other ways to compensate for their loss.

The Worker's Compensatory Options: The Federal/State Vocational Rehabilitation Program

The federal/state Vocational Rehabilitation Program provides work-related training and services to individuals who are potential workers or, more precisely, who are deemed employable by VR Program staff. Clients come to the program from many settings. Some have long work histories; others do not. Some are receiving cash benefits from private or public sources (like SSDI); others are not. What distinguishes VR clients is that they qualify for vocational rehabilitation on two counts: their disabilities prevent them from functioning successfully in the world of work, and there is reason to believe that VR services will correct this situation. In other words, VR clients are impaired enough to need help, but not so impaired as to be unemployable.

Unlike workers' compensation and SSDI, Vocational Rehabilitation is not an insurance program. Neither the recipient of VR services nor his employer pays into it directly. The federal/state VR Program receives 80 percent of its funds from general revenues allocated to the federal Rehabilitation Services Administration (RSA), located since 1980 in the Department of Education. RSA is charged in the Rehabilitation Act of 1973 with providing "wide-ranging services to assist disabled individuals to prepare for and engage in gainful occupations." The additional 20 percent of the program's funds are raised by the individual state agencies through which VR services are actually delivered.

The other important distinction between the VR Program and those described earlier in this chapter is that work history is not an eligibility requirement. Employment *potential* is the critical factor. Similarly, medically determinable disability is not the sole object of pre-admission evaluation. Employment potential is defined as partly attitudinal, and the VR counselor located in the state agency must judge an individual's psychic "fit" with what the program has to offer (interviews with MRC staff). In other words, work is no longer the "revelatory sign"; a desire to work is.

The Federal/State Vocational Rehabilitation Program's Array

In Figure 6, the VR Program is depicted as offering compensation at both the environmental and personal levels and through the social as well as the physical environment. All of the program's compensatory options are work-related, and environmental modification must facilitate the client's employment: the VR agency might modify clients' homes to make it easier for them to come and go, or adapt their vehicles so that they can transport themselves to and from work. The funds committed to environmental technologies are sub-

90

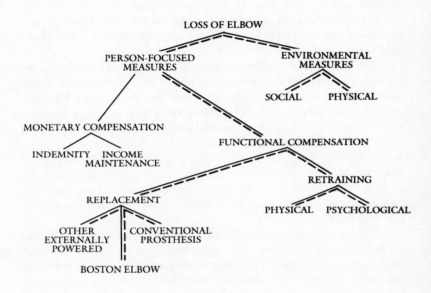

THE WORKER'S COMPENSATORY ARRAY:
VOCATIONAL REHABILITATION
Figure 6

stantial. In fiscal year 1982, for example, the Massachusetts Rehabilitation Commission allocated almost half a million of the less than $10 million spent on all client services to modification of the physical environment. The average sum spent on each adaptive housing recipient was over $3,000 and that spent on every vehicle modification client was more than $6,000 (MRC, 1983, pp. 7, 11). MRC does not make environmental changes in the workplace, but the agency will evaluate a client's potential work setting and make recommendations for modification to his or her prospective employer (interview with MRC staffer).

The VR client's social environment also changes. First, he or she forms a relationship with a rehabilitation counselor who acts as an advocate. This relationship is intended to be a source of support for the client while he or she adjusts to disability. The rehabilitation counselor also secures access to other professionals, vocational training programs, and the world of work generally. A second kind of social adaptation has been achieved through Section 503 of the Rehabilitation Act of 1973. This landmark legislation calls for, among other things, affirmative action by the federal government and its contractors. Federal agencies and all firms holding federal contracts for at least $2,500 are required to take affirmative action in hiring and promoting people with disabilities. Employers are expected to make a "reasonable accommodation" to the special needs of disabled employees, and workers or potential workers may file complaints against employers if they feel their rights have been violated. In fiscal year 1981, almost 2,500 such complaints were filed, approximately half dealing with hiring and half with firing. In the same year, nearly as many cases were closed, and 280 disabled individuals received something over $1 million in back pay as a result (RSA, 1982, p. 95). This is not a staggering figure, but it is still significant, for the 1973 legislation added a rights strategy to the rehabilitation services of long standing. This law will be explored at greater length in Chapter 4.

Monetary compensation is not a part of the VR Program array. Many clients do receive monetary benefits, but the public sources of these monies are generally SSDI or SSI. The real cash benefit of Vocational Rehabilitation is wages, and these are the unambiguous goal of the VR Program. "Rehabilitation" is itself defined for program purposes as employment in the competitive labor market or a sheltered work setting. The number of successful VR clients nationally was about 256,000 in fiscal year 1981. They represented 62 percent of the cases closed that year. This means that thirty-eight percent of the clients who finished the program were unable to find jobs they could do and keep (RSA, 1982, p. 13). MRC rehabilitated slightly more than 4,600 individuals in fiscal year 1982. Over 1,300 of them had been receiving some kind of public assistance (MRC, 1983, pp. 6c, 27), and these people represent a savings for government. The VR Program generally derives its legitimacy from the number of wage-earners it contributes to the economy. The rehabilitation literature is replete with cost-benefit analyses indicating that vocational rehabilitation is a good investment. Not surprisingly, none has isolated the effect of externally powered elbow prostheses. Still, if the Boston Elbow can be linked with employment, the VR Program is mandated to bear its cost.

Functional compensation is at the heart of the federal/state VR Program, and VR agencies may provide or contract for a complement of services. The first is evaluation and, if appropriate, intake. Then the client enters rehabilitation counseling, an ongoing relationship between a disabled individual and the rehabilitation professional who manages his or her case. Psychological counseling on work-related issues may also be available. A third kind of service is physical or occupational therapy. Another is actual vocational training in the form of schooling or on-the-job instruction. In some cases, the VR agency also provides support services—that is, services that make it possible for a client to take advantage of vocational training: personal care services, tools and supplies for occupational start-ups, day care for the client's children, and house and vehicular modification. Finally, when the course of training has been completed, the counselor undertakes the difficult task of job placement. According to one student of rehabilitation, the counselor is basically "a broker of sorts . . . matching the skills and competencies of the disabled person with the needs of society." A counselor must make his client "'saleable' in the economy" (Sussman, 1965, p. 209) and then must act as advocate for the sale.

Replacement has always been a compensatory option of the VR

Program, although in fiscal year 1975, only 9 percent of all VR clients received a prosthetic or orthotic device at an average cost of only $220 (Levitan and Taggart, 1977, p. 38). The role of replacement in vocational rehabilitation is to restore the functioning necessary for employment, and the VR Program may choose to pay for any device that achieves this end. But the program seems to operate without a complete understanding of the role of hardware in the rehabilitation process. Nor is there an explicit policy regarding the distribution of compensatory technology though the VR Program (interviews with past and present VR officials and staff). RSA's predecessor agency was at one time charged with promoting the development of technologies for vocational rehabilitation. The Rehabilitation Act of 1973 turned RSA's research unit into the National Institute of Handicapped Research (NIHR) and charged it with funding and overseeing research and development for medical, vocational, and recreational technologies. NIHR became the center of non-VA federal activity in these areas, and when RSA relocated in the Department of Education, NIHR was made a separate agency, a sister agency to RSA. NIHR's mandate is larger than that of the federal/state VR Program, extending to non-vocational rehabilitation, and although RSA and NIHR reportedly have a close relationship, NIHR does not and cannot be expected to generate policy about the role of technology in work specifically (interviews with RSA and NIHR officials).

At the state level, the Massachusetts Rehabilitation Commission is in the process of drafting guidelines for counselors to use in providing compensatory devices to their clients. A recent version indicates no major departure from or clarification of the program's basic stance: providing, in a cost-conscious manner, whatever the client needs to become employable. MRC does distribute rehabilitation technology, frequently covering the difference between the cost of a device and what a client's health insurance will pay—for example, the additional 20 percent required of Medicare beneficiaries. The agency has even purchased a Boston Elbow (interviews with Liberty Mutual and MRC staff). But one high-level MRC official expressed pointed skepticism about complex technologies for people with disabilities. He doubts their utility, especially when, as in the case of externally powered elbows, the devices are quite imperfect. This official traced mechanical insufficiencies to academic engineers who, he believes, are more interested in the technical challenges a device presents than in its ultimate usefulness (interview).

Whatever stance a VR agency takes vis-à-vis rehabilitation hardware is likely to affect the use of compensatory technologies by VR clients. Rehabilitation counselors provide not only funds for but information about assistive devices, including how desirable they are as a compensatory strategy. A counselor's own knowledge of and comfort with technology are likely to influence how and when the client uses it (Brown and Redden, 1979). It was argued in Chapter 1 that compensation for functional loss is never complete and that some of its aspects must be attended to to the exclusion of others. The choice of a compensatory technology, then, is a sorting out of aspects. It is highly subjective, sometimes ideological, and to the extent that the rehabilitation counselor makes that choice, he or she defines the client's view of his or her own disability. Two disability activists interviewed for this study (who disagreed about many other things) both contended that counselors as a group resist the introduction of technology into their practice. One activist believes that rehabilitation professionals are simply unwilling to accommodate technical change. The other emphasized the counselor's mistrust of complex and costly approaches to seemingly straightforward problems. A generalization offered by one long-time rehabilitation professional subsumes both versions: counselors view the rehabilitation process as an essentially human interaction, and they feel uneasy about expending dollars on, and relinquishing their role to, a machine (interview). There is an ironic symmetry here. Those who would diffuse rehabilitation technology through medical programs must identify compensatory devices with the strict materialism of "medical necessity"; those who look to VR for funding must convince rehabilitation counselors that a machine can be more personal than the sum of its mechanical parts.

The Federal/State Vocational Rehabilitation Program and the Boston Elbow

It is estimated that there are fifteen million people with physical disabilities in the United States, more than half of whom are not employed (Bowe, 1980, cited in OTA, 1982, p. 101). Many of these are potential VR clients. In fiscal year 1981, the basic Vocational Rehabilitation Program was funded at about $1.05 billion. This figure represented a decrease of 10 percent in real terms from fiscal year 1980 and a real decrease for the sixth year in a row. The VR Program shows signs of strain. "New cases, caseload levels and the number of persons served and rehabilitated all shrank to volumes last seen in the period from Fiscal Year 1969 to Fiscal Year 1971" (RSA, 1982, p. 11). The only indicators to increase were the number of persons not accepted into the VR Program and the number of persons who, once accepted, were not rehabilitated (RSA, 1982, pp. 9, 8b). MRC enjoyed a fiscal year 1981 increase in state funds while federal funds were falling off. In fiscal year 1982, both sources decreased their contribution to program operation (MRC, 1983, p. 7).

A second constraint on the VR Program is its relatively recent redirection of services toward the "severely disabled." The Rehabilitation Act of 1973 first targeted people with severe disabilities for vocational rehabilitation. The legislation was drafted in response to severely disabled activists who charged that VR agencies inflated their rehabilitation rates by "skimming" the least needy clients off the top of the applicant pool. Demands for a new bill were apparently justified. The mandate of the Vocational Rehabilitation Program had been to put disabled people to work, but rehabilitation counselors interpreted this narrowly, accepting only the least disabled clients in the belief that they would be easiest to place (interview with two former federal rehabilitation commissioners and state VR staff). The practice of skimming has a long history in social welfare practice (see, for example, Scott, 1969) and at least in part derives from an agency's need to demonstrate its effectiveness. According to a former commissioner of RSA, however, skimming also reflected an "almost religious belief" by VR counselors that severely disabled people could not be rehabilitated to compete for employment in the marketplace (interview). The Rehabilitation Act of 1973 was a symbolic refutation of this belief, and the program does appear to have been reoriented. Virtually every VR-related interview done for this study yielded anecdotal data about an influx of severely disabled clients. In addition, RSA reported that although the decline in caseload and other indicators noted above did affect the severely dis-

abled, the effects on less disabled clients were much greater. Fiscal
year 1981 saw the largest proportion of severely disabled clients in
the eight years for which such a statistic was kept (RSA, 1982, p.
14). In Massachusetts, people with severe disabilities accounted for
80 percent of all rehabilitations in fiscal year 1982. This was the
highest proportion in at least the previous five years, although in absolute terms, 1980 was a better year for this client group (MRC,
1983, p. 6c).

According to the Rehabilitation Services Administration, insufficient funds and more severely disabled clients have contributed to
the decline in successful rehabilitations (RSA, 1982, p. 8). It is possible that these factors work against diffusion of the Boston Elbow
too. Although the loss of an arm above the elbow is considered a severe disability, MRC's Office for the Severely Disabled has a
caseload exclusively of clients in wheelchairs. The head of that office
explained that, until the early 1970s, individuals with spinal-cord injuries were rarely accepted into the VR Program, mostly because
program staff thought they were too disabled to find employment.
Many of these same individuals were instrumental in the enactment
of the 1973 Rehabilitation Act, and when the Act produced an influx of clients with spinal-cord injuries, the Office for the Severely
Disabled was created to assist them. The office has since expanded its
clientele to include people with muscular dystrophy, cerebral palsy,
and head injuries (interviews). Still, all of these clients are wheelchair
users and focus the office's attention on issues of physical accessibility. A second and related point is that technological responses to
spinal-cord injury may be very costly. Body-powered wheelchairs are
a relatively inexpensive option for some clients with spinal-cord injuries. And even electric wheelchairs are sometimes covered by Medicare and Medicaid. But "medically necessary" chairs are often inadequate for vocational goals, and the higher the spinal-cord injury, the
more compensation the wheelchair must provide. Wheelchairs also
bring other technologies in their wake—home and vehicle modification, for example.

Wheelchair users and persons with above-elbow amputations
have much in common. They are severely disabled. Their disabilities
are to some extent technologically remediable. They sometimes present the VR Program with choices between more and less sophisti-

cated compensatory technologies. But potential wearers of the Boston Elbow are also different from their mobility-impaired counterparts. They are far fewer in number. The head of MRC's Office for the Severely Disabled estimates that there are 10,000 persons with spinal-cord injuries in Massachusetts alone (interview) in comparison with 50,000 persons with above-elbow amputations nationally. And most people with amputations have serviceable "low"-technology alternatives to the Boston Elbow: a cable-operated device or no device at all. Furthermore, the loss of lower-extremity function generally requires environmental measures as well as a wheelchair. High spinal-cord injury may call for the most elaborate sort of machine. Under these conditions, the perceived *marginal* utility of the Boston Elbow becomes a consideration. Is the Elbow enough of an improvement over body-powered arms to justify its increased cost to the VR Program? Is its advantage over alternative prostheses greater than the advantage of, say, an electric wheelchair over its alternative? Is the Boston Elbow perceived as more advantageous? Persons with above-elbow amputations are relatively rare, and the fine points of myoelectric prosthetics are less well known to decision-makers than is the benefit of a quadriplegic client's sip-and-puff wheelchair.

To summarize, the Boston Elbow may diffuse through the federal/state Vocational Rehabilitation Program, especially since both the Elbow and the program are designed to put disabled people back to work. The scope of the VR mandate coupled with fiscal constraints and competing constituencies makes it less likely but by no means impossible for the person with an above-elbow amputation who is a potential worker to be provided by the VR Program with a Boston Elbow.

The Worker's Compensatory Options:
   Conclusions

The worker who has suffered an amputation has three sets of compensatory options, each addressed to a different set of circumstances.

The mechanisms by which these options are delivered also differ, and the programs described above vary across several dimensions: eligibility requirements, financing, kinds of compensation
offered, and, more abstractly, the way in which amputation is construed.

Eligibility for workers' compensation insurance extends to almost every worker injured in the workplace. The program is financed largely through private insurance companies, who sell coverage to employers and respond to legitimate claims with the options
(subject to state variations) pictured in Figure 4. Under workers'
compensation, income maintenance and functional measures are ultimately mutually exclusive—restoration of upper-extremity function relieves the insurer of part of his or her financial responsibility
to the worker—and this arrangement is an incentive to provide the
Boston Elbow. But these insurers are competitors for workers' compensation clients. Liberty Mutual has little incentive to diffuse the
device to other firms, and they in turn resist becoming Liberty Mutual customers.

Eligibility for Social Security Disability Insurance is limited to
totally disabled individuals who as workers have paid into the Social
Security system. Employees and employers finance SSDI with payroll taxes, and beneficiaries co-pay for Medicare services. SSDI provides the compensatory options pictured in Figure 5. The program
offers less than workers' compensation does, because its primary purpose is only to maintain financially and medically those workers who
cannot return to work. SSDI monetary benefits are solely income-
maintenance payments, and the functional compensation pictured
above does not begin until the beneficiary has received monetary
compensation for twenty-four months. The Elbow may appear in
this array, but only if Medicare officials perceive the prosthesis as
medically necessary.

Eligibility for the federal/state VR Program is extended to all
disabled individuals with the potential to work. It is financed primarily with federal revenues allocated to the Rehabilitation Services
Administration and then to state rehabilitation agencies. According
to Figure 6, the VR Program is complementary to SSDI. In fact,
SSDI refers beneficiaries with employment potential to VR, and

conversely many VR clients receive SSDI benefits. The Boston Elbow is well suited to the VR Program and has been provided in this
context at least once. But Figure 6 also reveals a bias toward interpersonal responses to disability. Of the three arrays pictured in this
chapter, only the one shown in Figure 6 incorporates social compensation at the environmental level and psychological compensation at
the personal. Moreover, severely disabled people have become a priority of the program, and the Boston Elbow is only one of the many
expensive technologies appropriate for this clientele.

Persons with amputations are among the clients of all three programs, but amputation seems to be understood differently in each.
Workers' compensation beneficiaries have suffered a finite loss, one
that can be measured for the purposes of an indemnity in finite dollar amounts. By losing an arm, these workers have lost a tool of their
trade, and they are paid income maintenance based on their pre-
injury wages until they can earn that sum themselves. For SSDI, amputation is a total disability, the only kind of disability the program
acknowledges. The recipient is therefore provided with the staples of
modern life: income and medical care. The subtleties of functionality
are lost on SSDI, and Medicare, as a benefit for long-term recipients
only, does not contribute to a worker's initial adaptation to functional loss. The federal/state VR Program is the most complete in its
understanding of amputation. Although monetary compensation is
left to SSDI, the rehabilitation agency will intervene if necessary in
every other way. Amputation even in this work-oriented program is
construed to have social and psychological aspects, in part as a result
of the VR Program's professional norms. Interpersonal relationships
and civil rights legislation may also be less expensive or less patroni-
zing ways respectively to place people with disabilities in jobs. In any
case, the VR Program serves a client with physical and social needs
and, ironically, this may not work to the advantage of the Boston
Elbow.

The dominant models of technological innovation are inadequate to reveal these ironies. They neither incorporate alternatives to
the Boston Elbow nor distinguish among classes of users. Government acts differently in relation to past, present, and potential workers and designs its compensatory strategies accordingly. These mea-

sures may include the Boston Elbow, but they rarely focus on the device. Here, as in Chapter 2, diffusion of the Boston Elbow is most thoroughly understood in the context of its alternatives and the kinds of users to whom it is distributed.

4
The Body Politic
The Citizen

The citizen discussed in this chapter is any American who loses an arm. Like his or her veteran and worker counterpart, he or she is offered an array of compensatory measures, personal and environmental. First, low-income citizens with amputations are eligible for the Supplemental Security Income (SSI) program, which in most states includes Medicaid benefits. Eligibility for the program depends not on the person's status as veteran or worker but on disability and low income alone. The citizen's environmental options are not means-tested. They consist, rather, of research on and regulation of rehabilitation technologies, and a set of policies that make society more accessible to people with disabilities. Research and regulation modulate market forces to ensure the availability and safety of rehabilitation devices. Policies that promote accessibility alter the environment to compensate the individual for his or her disability. Eligibility for the second group of measures is universal. The person with an amputation need not be a veteran or worker. Of course the citizen with an amputation may be a veteran or worker, and veterans and workers are citizens too. Still, some citizens fall into no other category. The compensatory options described in this chapter accrue to them.

One might expect to find the Boston Elbow in the citizen's array. Medicaid is the largest public means-tested medical program in the United States. The National Institute of Handicapped Research (NIHR) has an explicit mandate to provide technological responses to disability, and the rehabilitation legislation of 1973 and 1978 calls for the full integration of people with severe disabilities. The Boston Elbow is not, however, likely to appear in this array. Benefits at the personal level are provided through the welfare system, which disdains expensive purchases and requires that prostheses be "medically necessary." Research at NIHR has too broad a mandate and too small an appropriation to contribute much to the Boston Elbow's use. Finally, policies that create access to the American mainstream operate at the environmental level, reorienting rehabilitation efforts away from personal assistive devices. These are countervailing forces to government's diffusion of the Boston Elbow.

The Citizen's Array

Look for a moment at Figure 7, which depicts compensatory options of the low-income citizen with an amputation. First, disabled individuals may be eligible for Supplemental Security Income (SSI), a program that provides income maintenance to poor people whose disabilities are total and expected to last at least twelve months or to result in death. In 1980, 4.2 million such people were receiving SSI payments at a cost to the federal government of $7.9 billion. States are free to supplement this federal benefit ($2,856 per recipient in 1980), and every state but Texas does (Kennedy, 1982, pp. 3, 9).

SSI mirrors Social Security Disability Insurance in some important ways. SSI recipients must be totally disabled over the same twelve-month period. Total disability is defined again as the inability to engage in "substantial gainful activity," and vocational as well as health factors figure in determining eligibility for the program. Another similarity is that responsibility for SSI determination lies with the state vocational rehabilitation agency, which receives federal funding for this purpose. Unlike SSDI, SSI does not require recipients to have contributed to the program in the past, nor in fact to have worked at all. It is funded through general revenues and serves clients solely on the basis of an individual's disability and income.

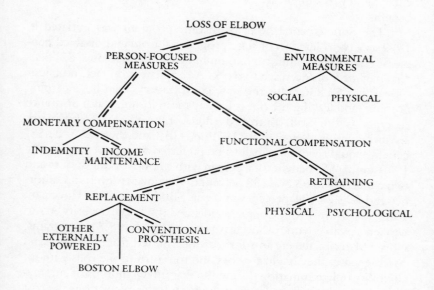

THE CITIZEN'S COMPENSATORY ARRAY I
Figure 7

The unmarried SSI beneficiary without dependents can earn no more than the sum of his or her federal and state payments. Recipients' money earnings are deducted dollar for dollar from their benefits.

The Supplemental Security Income program was initiated in 1972 as a consolidation of state programs for old and disabled people; it established a uniform minimum benefit across states. SSI benefits may be a disincentive to work. A recipient is, in fact, no better off earning $2,856 (plus the state contribution) than he is earning nothing, and leaving the SSI rolls may mean losing health insurance coverage as well. Still, controlled studies of the effect of SSI on work are inconclusive (Better et al., 1979, p. 413). and the size of the SSI benefit would seem too small to be preferred to regular wages. The 1979 annual SSI benefit for a person with a non-working spouse and two children was $3,864 (58 percent of the poverty level) in California and $2,273 (34 percent) in Texas (Burkhauser and Haveman, 1982, p. 58). In 1980, Congress amended the Social Security Act to weaken possible work disincentives in the SSI and SSDI programs. Now SSI recipients are in some cases permitted to retain Medicaid coverage after they begin to work and to return to the rolls without eligibility redetermination during the first fifteen months of employment. The amendment also excludes from wage calculations the cost of certain disability expenses related to work, prosthetic devices among them. The SSI beneficiary might buy a Boston Elbow under these conditions, but it probably remains a prohibitively expensive option for someone on the SSI program.

The citizen who is eligible for SSI may receive functional compensation through the Medicaid program. Medicaid is in this respect comparable to the Medicare benefits that accompany SSDI, but there are also important differences. First, Medicaid pays 100 percent of a beneficiary's (covered) medical expenses—that is, there is no deductible for him or her to pay. Neither must the beneficiary wait to begin receiving Medicaid benefits; they are coupled with SSI payments from the start. Furthermore, Medicaid is a state-administered program, varying considerably from state to state, and while prosthetic and rehabilitation services may be among a state's Medicaid benefits, they do not have to be.

In Massachusetts, the Medicaid program does provide prosthetic devices. The medical necessity of any one prosthesis for any one person must be established by a physician at a Medicaid-approved clinic, and because the Boston Elbow and other prostheses are not scheduled for Medicaid by the rate-setting commission, they must receive "prior approval" from program officials before they can be provided to Medicaid recipients. According to the Medicaid officials and private prosthetists interviewed for this study, the decision to grant prior approval is highly discretionary and rests on the strength of the prescribing physician's argument that the device is "medically justified" in a particular case. This represents a departure from regulations concerning durable medical equipment, which is approved only when not "substantially more costly than medically appropriate and feasible alternatives" (Massachusetts Medicaid, 1981). Medicaid officials claim they would seriously consider approving a request for a Boston Elbow if it were *medically* indicated (interviews). Still, it seems unlikely that Medicaid, "welfare medicine" (Stevens and Stevens, 1974), would purchase a prosthesis as costly in both absolute and relative terms as the Boston Elbow. An exception might be made in the case of someone with a very high amputation that precludes use of a cable-operated device.

Distribution of prosthetics under the Medicaid program is achieved through the personal operating principles of program officials and medical professionals. One Medicaid official reported that he practices a kind of triage with requests for very costly devices. He would respond differently, for example, to two requests for an electric wheelchair if one were for an elderly patient and the other for a child. He would consider the child the better investment. Similarly, he "winds down" requests for expensive items: he will buy a hospital bed but not a top-of-the-line mattress for it (interview). Among prescribing physicians, a third principle is to request what is likely to be approved. Medicaid has a reputation for expending its resources conservatively, and this produces a kind of "chilling effect" in the rehabilitation community. One physician explained that he simply does not prescribe what he does not expect to get—that is, something more than the most basic compensatory technology—for his patients on Medicaid (interview). Finally, a physiatrist who both prescribes for Medicaid patients and has served as a medical consultant for the program made a personal effort to confront those who would inhibit his practice of rehabilitation medicine. He found program officials to be generally sympathetic but constrained by the legislature's reluctance to make Medicaid expenditures. This he lays at the door of the taxpayer, who evidently does not believe that the welfare budget is the place for sophisticated compensatory technology. As one disabled activist put it at a conference, "We have seen the enemy, and it is our next-door neighbors" (personal communication). This conflict will reappear in the discussion of disability rights below. Suffice it to say here that, at the personal level, the citizen's compensatory options are provided through the welfare system, an unlikely source for a Boston Elbow.

Figure 8 depicts the citizen's non-means-tested compensatory options. The first is federally funded disability research—not the provision of a Boston Elbow, but a setting in which this device and others can be researched, developed, and evaluated. The National Institute of Handicapped Research estimates that in fiscal year 1979 almost $66 million in federal monies went to disability research. Ten agencies expended these funds. NIHR, the Veterans Administration, the National Science Foundation, and the National Institutes of Health each had budgets of over $1 million for this kind of work (OTA, 1982, p. 60).

In 1977, an advisory panel to the House Committee on Science and Technology reported that the federal presence in disability research was poorly funded and organized and operating on insufficient information about disabled Americans (U.S. Congress, 1977). A second advisory panel followed in 1978, and its findings were similar, if more specific (U.S. Congress, 1978). Both panels were inclined toward the "lifecycle" view of compensatory technologies and gave this metaphor legitimacy. Both, while recommending a greater research role for the federal government, urged the creation of strong ties to the private sector. Government was cast as a facilitator at specific stages in the product lifecycle, not as a primary source of compensatory technology.

As noted above, the National Institute of Handicapped Research was created along these lines by the 1978 amendments to the Rehabilitation Act of 1973. The Institute was to serve as the federal entity having primary responsibility for disability research and was

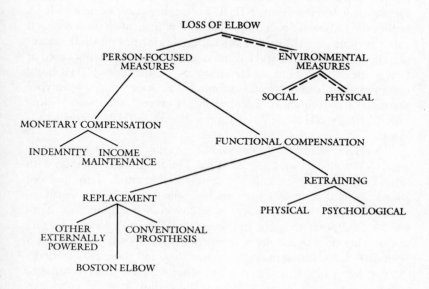

THE CITIZEN'S COMPENSATORY ARRAY II
Figure 8

fashioned from the research component of the Rehabilitation Services Administration. When in 1980 RSA was moved from the Department of Health, Education, and Welfare to the newly established Department of Education, NIHR was made a sister agency to RSA within the Office of Special Education. The Institute has no research capacity of its own. Rather, it sets national priorities for disability research and gives grants and contracts to researchers, usually based at universities, to carry out relevant projects. Neither does NIHR build compensatory technologies, although it does fund prototypes through Rehabilitation Engineering Centers, discussed below (RSA, 1982; NIHR, 1981; interview with NIHR scientific advisor).

NIHR's mandate is considerable, especially given its budget—$28 million in fiscal year 1982. The Institute is charged with attending to all "handicaps," physical and mental. This includes problems as diverse as schizophrenia, spinal-cord injury, deafness, cystic fibrosis, mental retardation, and of course amputation. It includes conditions, more or less severe, stable and degenerative, rare and common, that require a compensatory response. NIHR must formulate many different research strategies, and these call for methodological flexibility and expertise. Moreover, the sheer volume of needs about which NIHR worries is staggering. The agency's *Long-Range Plan,* issued in 1981, states four major goals, each subdivided into a number of objectives: "minimizing the incidence of disability and maximizing the functional capacities of handicapped individuals"; "improving employment prospects and alleviating problems of daily living"; "improving quality of service and systems of financial support"; and "populations of new concern" (NIHR, 1981, p. 27). (It is worth noting that the last of these goals is a reference to disabled people below the age of eighteen and above the age of sixty-five—that is, those who fall outside the traditional vocational rehabilitation clientele.) The Office of Technology Assessment rightly finds the NIHR research agenda "overwhelming" (OTA, 1982, p. 70).

The National Institute of Handicapped Research pursues its mandate in four ways: Research and Demonstration Projects; Research and Training Centers (RTCs); Rehabilitation Engineering Centers (RECs); and Research Utilization Projects. RTCs received the largest part, 52 percent, of NIHR's funding in fiscal year 1981 and have been a component of the federal rehabilitation system since 1962. In 1981 there were twenty-three RTCs, each focused on one of six areas of interest: medical research, mental illness, blindness, deafness, vocational rehabilitation, and mental retardation. Every center operates in conjunction with a university and may be associated with a rehabilitation services program. Many are situated in medical schools; all are designed to disseminate research findings through the training of rehabilitation professionals (RSA, 1982; NIHR, 1981).

Twenty-one percent of NIHR's fiscal year 1979 budget went to Rehabilitation Engineering Centers, the NIHR component most likely to do prosthetics research. RECs are more directly involved with hardware and must be located in clinical rehabilitation facilities, where center staff design and build prototypical equipment-embodied technologies. Improved prostheses, including externally powered above-elbow prostheses, are an explicit objective in NIHR's *Long-Range Plan*. Arm researchers received monies from NIHR's predecessor agency, and in fiscal year 1983, the Institute funded an REC doing research relevant to the Boston Elbow (interviews with rehabilitation engineers and RSA staffer). Still, prosthetics is only one of the agency's fourteen areas of "prioritized technology research." An appendix to the *Plan,* moreover, explains that externally powered elbows "have not made a significant impact" because persons with amputations can function "very well" with one arm and therefore value cosmesis over functionality in a prosthesis (NIHR, 1981, p. 10). NIHR is at best too busy to diffuse the Boston Elbow. At worst, it does not consider the device worthy of diffusion.

Related to federal research and development is the regulation of medical devices by the Food and Drug Administration; while NIHR stimulates diffusion, the FDA restrains it to ensure user safety. The 1976 amendments to the Food, Drug, and Cosmetic Act (also known as the Medical Devices Amendments) apply to prostheses insofar as they are, in Congress' words, "intended to affect the structure or any function of the body of man or other animals." The amendments charge the FDA with regulating the safety and effectiveness of all medical devices, and because the range of technologies denoted by the term is wide, the FDA has been equipped with differ-

ent regulatory mechanisms for different kinds of machines. Medical
devices are classified I, II, or III, depending on whether they require
general controls (least regulation), performance standards, or pre-
market approval (most regulation) respectively. Classification rests
on two criteria: how important a device claims to be in sustaining
life or preventing impairment of health, and how great the potential
is for the device to cause illness or injury. In 1980, Victor Zafra, then
acting director of the Bureau of Medical Devices, described the classification system as an instance of "responsible regulatory reform"
(Zafra, 1980, p. 9). By this he meant that the FDA would respect
significant differences among devices and the rights of manufacturers not to be more heavily regulated than necessary.

Upper-extremity prostheses are subject to Class I controls, including prohibition of adulterated or misbranded products, bans on
particular devices, and an insistence on good manufacturing practices as defined by the agency. These controls apply as long as the
prosthetics manufacturer sells his or her product in component
parts, that is, through prosthetists who assemble it. According to officials at the FDA and the American Orthotics and Prosthetics Association, prosthetics manufacturers and practitioners proposed the
Class I designation, and the FDA's Surgical and Rehabilitation Devices Panel, which was responsible for classifying limb prostheses,
approved it. Political pressure need not be inferred here. The very
nature of limb prostheses suggests Class I controls. Artificial limbs
are for the most part distributed to patients through prosthetics
practitioners who are as much craftsmen as health professionals—
who are likely to discern dangerous imperfections in devices that
they assemble. Unlike some medical devices, limb prostheses are also
worn externally. They remain in sight at all times and do not intrude
upon the user's anatomy or body chemistry. Finally, prostheses do
not purport to sustain life nor prevent impairment of health, so, on
the FDA's own terms, the Boston Elbow and its prosthetic alternatives do not demand the closest attention. As long as prostheses remain Class I devices, the FDA will play a minor role in their diffusion.

The citizen with an amputation is also entitled to the environmental compensation provided by the rehabilitation legislation of

1973 and 1978. The Rehabilitation Act of 1973 (P.L. 93-112) made significant changes in both the human and built environments. Its goal was to create for people with disabilities points of access to the American mainstream.

Section 502 of the Act created the Architectural and Transportation Barriers Compliance Board, which is mandated to ensure the physical accessibility of federal buildings and those built with federal funds since 1968. Together with legislation treating mass transportation (P.L. 91-453 and P.L. 93-391) and highways (P.L. 93-87), Section 502 was a product of the "barrier-free movement," which began in the late 1950s. In 1958, the federal government published a guide to making public buildings accessible to people with mobility impairments. In 1961, a more comprehensive standard was issued by a private architectural standard-setting organization and was widely endorsed. Still, compliance was only voluntary, and the National Commission on Architectural Barriers to Rehabilitation of the Handicapped found in 1965 that federally funded construction was still producing inaccessible buildings. In 1968, the Architectural Barriers Act was passed. Its provisions were much like those of the 1973 legislation but did not include an enforcement mechanism. Section 502 addressed this weakness by granting the Architectural and Tranportation Barriers Compliance Board the power to issue compliance orders and to call on the courts for enforcement when necessary (DeJong and Lifchez, 1983). Although physical accessibility is not directly relevant to persons with above-elbow amputations, some scholars ascribe a larger significance to Section 502: "By declaring that living in a barrier-free environment is a fundamental 'right' of disabled people, the government for the first time stated its intent to adjust social norms to accommodate the handicapped, rather than to provide assistance to the handicapped in their efforts to adjust to social norms" (Burkhauser and Haveman, 1982, p. 100).

Section 503 of the Rehabilitation Act requires federal agencies and contractors to take affirmative action in hiring and promoting people with disabilities. The law is designed to create access to a social environment, namely the world of work, but prospective employers are expected to make a "reasonable accommodation" to all of the disabled employee's special needs and this may mean modifying the physical plant as well. In this study, 503 appears in the worker's rather than the citizen's array. It pertains only to conditions of employment and has been discussed in Chapter 3.

Section 504 of P.L. 93-112 is potentially the most powerful. It prohibits discrimination against people with disabilities by federal agencies and by organizations receiving federal aid of any kind. Section 504 applies to all activity, including education, health care, social services, and federally assisted employment. The Reagan administration has proposed significant changes in the regulations implementing the law, and the resulting discord represents the most important battle for accessibility at the federal level. Since 1980, Justice Department staff attorneys have repeatedly pitted themselves against Reagan appointees in interpreting the Rehabilitation Act of 1973. Still in dispute is perhaps the single most critical issue in implementing Section 504: whether organizations and institutions receiving federal aid are prohibited from discriminating against people with disabilities in all programs and services or only in those receiving federal aid (*New York Times,* April 26, 1983; interview with head of national disability rights organization). The Reagan administration has proposed the latter interpretation in draft regulations, and in March 1984 the Supreme Court gave a similar reading to sex discrimination legislation. During a meeting with federal officials in May 1982, a predominantly disabled audience reacted angrily to an explication of the New Federalism. One activist exhorted those assembled to "walk out or crawl out or roll out," and they did (*New York Times,* April 26, 1983). Final action has yet to be taken on the regulations for Section 504, and implementation is being complicated further by competing definitions of accessibility. Specifically, can an organization be socially accessible if it is not physically accessible, and if not, how much physical modification does Section 504 require (Meislin, 1981)? Resolution of these issues will not affect diffusion of the Boston Elbow directly. It will, however, make environmental alternatives more or less feasible and effective.

In addition to being an environmental strategy for dealing with functional loss, P.L. 93-112 for the first time targeted people with severe disabilities for rehabilitation services. The federal/state Vocational Rehabilitation Program had, as noted in Chapter 3, served this clientele badly, and in the early 1970s, severely disabled people succeeded in pressing their claims against the rehabilitation system. They became the expressed priority of the VR Program. Still, vocational goals were unrealistic for many people with severe disabilities, and the 1978 amendments to the Rehabilitation Act expanded the rehabilitation mandate to include services unrelated to work.

Title VII of the amendments provides for state rehabilitation agencies to establish independent living centers (ILCs) where severely disabled people without the potential for employment can be assisted to live as independently as possible. This legislation issued from the independent living movement, which began in the early 1970s among disabled people living in institutions. Movement founders believed that even people with very serious impairments could, with training and support, live in a deinstitutionalized setting; the ILC was designed to provide whatever services might prove necessary for attaining maximum independence (DeJong and Lifchez, 1983). Independent living centers modify the disabled person's living conditions. Although ILC staff do help individuals to change, they more often work with the client to modify his or her environment. The ethos of the independent living movement is that it is the world that needs changing. Less emphasis is placed on altering the disabled person through prosthetic devices.

The ILC is typified by the Boston Center for Independent Living (BCIL), which was one of the first such centers in the United States and pre-dated the 1978 amendments by two years. Funded by private as well as public sources, BCIL has a staff of about thirty and a fluid clientele, most of whom are mobility-impaired. BCIL provides assistance in finding and securing adapted housing, information about transportation, recreation, and counseling, training in homemaking and financial management, advocacy with government agencies and the legislatures, and self-help adjustment, a kind of peer counseling (interview with BCIL staff).

But Title VII has never been fully funded. Federal and state monies have been made available for the establishment and operation of ILCs, including training, advocacy, and outreach, but not for the purchase of services *per se*. Thus BCIL receives no Title VII funds to use in actually adapting a client's environment, although the Center garners money for this purpose from other sources. The Massachusetts Medicaid program and the Department of Mental Health, for example, contract with BCIL to run transitional living facilities where clients learn to live independently in supervised congregate residences. In some cases a personal care attendant—someone to help with daily activities like bathing, dressing, and eating—is also provided as part of the transitional environment. But these programs are open only to Medicaid and Department of Mental Health clients. BCIL clients who do not fall into these categories do not receive this service. Similarly, BCIL is not funded to provide compensatory technologies, although Center staff might evaluate the usefulness of some device for a particular client, direct him or her to the source of the technology, and assist him or her in securing funds for it (interview with BCIL staff). Coverage decisions made in other programs are thus highly relevant to the availability of devices to clients, and the Boston Elbow is unlikely to diffuse through the program.

The Citizen and the Boston Elbow

The citizen with an amputation has both person-focused and environmental compensatory options. Different measures obtain under different circumstances; for example, income maintenance and medical benefits are provided to poor clients only. The other options described in this chapter, however, are distinguished less by the subgroup of citizens to whom they are offered than by the conception of the citizen on which they are based. This chapter's compensatory strategies represent three views of the relationship between government and the individual. First, the poor citizen is provided with subsistence benefits that may be technological in form. Second, the government stimulates and polices the market for technology where citizens act as buyers and sellers. Finally, the disabled citizen is understood as less than equal in a society of equals, and technology emerges as one way to reconstitute him. Each of these conceptions raises different issues for technology as a compensatory measure.

This chapter began with a discussion of Supplemental Security Income and Medicaid. Options for low-income clients, these programs derive from poor law; they offer minimal income maintenance and health care that is "medically necessary." SSI is an income floor. Recipients are entitled to the difference between their incomes and the SSI level set by the federal and state governments. Every dollar earned is deducted from benefits paid, and the maximum a beneficiary is allowed to earn is still less than the federal poverty level (Bowe, 1980, cited in OTA, 1982, p. 105).

Similarly, Medicaid is welfare medicine. The federal government requires that participating states provide basic medical services, but the inclusion of prosthetics is optional. States that provide prostheses, moreover, are free to regulate their distribution, and there is evidence that Medicaid officials are reluctant to spend more than they have to to make medically necessary interventions. The poor client, then, is entitled to a modest compensatory strategy. He or she is considered to be among the "deserving poor" by virtue of the amputation and does receive minimal income maintenance and health care. He or she is not, however, likely to wear a Boston Elbow. The poor citizen is too poor to purchase one, and state Medicaid programs are generally unlikely to judge the Boston Elbow medically necessary.

The compensatory options of the low-income citizen with an amputation are not meant to be restorative. Government provides neither an incentive for nor conditions conducive to a return to pre-amputation status. Rather, disability is viewed as an unfortunate occurrence whose effects can be blunted by the social welfare system; it is a loss of function and income for which government and no one else can be made to pay. Under these conditions, any compensatory technology will raise questions about absolute cost to public programs and its cost relative to other devices and non-mechanical means to the same end. The Boston Elbow is both quite costly in an absolute sense and, at least in the view of some, too costly for the marginal benefit it provides. It is not compatible with the first conception of the citizen.

A second kind of policy for the citizen with an amputation pertains primarily to the market. It comprises two environmental measures—research and development by NIHR and other federal agencies and regulation by the FDA. Although the former serves to stimulate economic activity and the latter to restrain it, both efforts treat prosthetics as a market good. An artificial arm is essentially a product, and the person who uses it (or his or her agent) is essentially a consumer.

The federal government does not produce prosthetics, but it does have an interest in their production, and although compensatory devices are ultimately secured in the private sector, government mitigates through research and development funding the probable unprofitability of compensatory technologies. Like "orphan drugs," many technologies for people with disabilities have relatively small numbers of potential buyers. Above-elbow prostheses, for example, have a maximum domestic market of 50,000. Disability is also idiosyncratic and embedded, and the general utility of any compensatory device is often limited. There are, moreover, high research costs associated with rehabilitation technologies. The impairments that underlie disabilities may not be well understood, and appropriate research subjects may be hard to find. Government takes on some of these costs to keep the market functioning.

The involvement of the FDA in diffusing prosthetics is similar to that of the research agencies. Medical devices have the potential for great good and great harm and may be bought and sold safely only with regulatory intervention. But while the FDA polices the market, it does not call into question the basic organization of economic activity. Rather, regulation, like research, posits a disabled consumer to whom rehabilitation technologies may be distributed through the market. In the case of the Boston Elbow, neither the FDA nor NIHR strongly influences diffusion. They do, however, represent a second conception of the citizen, one where amputation creates the need for an arm and there is the expectation that the market will provide it. Functional loss does not change the consumer in any basic way. It merely adds compensatory technology to his or her shopping list.

The third conception of the citizen with an amputation is as less than equal in a world of equals. Unlike the first version of citizenship, in which public programs shelter the poor, or the second, which charges government with seeing that the market functions, the third conception is expressly political. Here disability is an impairment of the body politic. If the American polity comprises equal individuals, who are free to pursue personal ends and to advocate for their interests in setting collective goals, functional loss is not simply a personal contingency with which the state is expected to help. It is instead a threat to public life. Impairment may inhibit political participation, and the legislation of 1973 and 1978 was designed to guarantee disabled people a chance to participate.

Sections 502, 503, and 504 are three strategies for making society accessible to people with disabilities. They are meant to further the personal ends of disabled people by creating equal opportunity, at least in activities receiving federal funds. Similarly, the independent living program makes deinstitutionalization possible and thus provides people with disabilities with the opportunity to pursue personal goals in the mainstream. Equality of opportunity is a recurrent theme in discussions of disability policy, although its precise meaning varies from speaker to speaker. For some, it is rooted in the basic American belief in self-reliance. Gerben DeJong and Raymond Lifchez, for example, argue that the 1973 and 1978 legislation "has an affinity with the traditional non-interventionist values of the political right," particularly the belief that individuals should be permitted to "shape their own destiny" (DeJong and Lifchez, 1983, p. 40). Taking the argument a step further, George Will calls on the Reagan administration to demonstrate "subtlety in its conservatism" and act so as to communicate that, "although we conservatives believe government has been irrationally intrusive, we know that there are persons who cannot help themselves until government helps them. And we know there are conservative values that are not vivified until the government affirms them with strong regulations" (Will, 1983, p. 8).

Implementing a policy of self-help is more difficult than advocating it. The Education of All Handicapped Children Act of 1975, for example, established the right of a disabled child to a free, "appropriate" education in the "least restrictive environment." Much like the rehabilitation legislation of the 1970s, the act is distinguished from earlier education legislation in its emphasis on "access." In 1982, the parents of Amy Rowley, a deaf child who attended the local public school, charged that their school district had acted illegally in refusing to provide a sign-language interpreter for their daughter. The Rowleys argued that without the interpreter, the child would be unable to realize her full educational potential and that this constituted a violation of the Handicapped Education Act. The Supreme Court decided against the Rowleys in what was described as a "blow" to disability activism (Fiske, 1982). William Rehnquist, writing for the majority, explained that schools were required to provide disabled students with some compensation for functional loss, but not necessarily with enough compensation to develop their potential fully. Rehnquist interpreted the Handicapped Education Act as mandating a "basic floor of opportunity," not what the dissenting opinion termed "full opportunity." Writing for the minority, Byron White argued that the intent of the Act was to guarantee children with disabilities the same educational opportunities as able-bodied children and that this could only be achieved by eliminating the effects of functional loss. In Amy Rowley's case, only a sign-language interpreter could have restored the opportunity lost through her congenital deafness (Greenhouse, 1982). This judicial difference of opinion represents a fundamental disagreement about how much opportunity is enough. Must a school district provide a child who has suffered an amputation with the prosthesis that will maximize his or her opportunities to learn? A myoelectric elbow might allow a student to realize his or her potential in vocational education or laboratory science. A broad reading of the legislation might therefore indirectly stimulate diffusion of such a device.

The rehabilitation legislation of 1973 and 1978 seeks equal opportunity for disabled Americans. The independent living program affords people with severe disabilities greater opportunity to reside in the mainstream. The ILC also maximizes opportunities for self-care. Even clients who require help with daily activities such as bathing are given the chance to choose and train their personal care attendants. Section 502, similarly, is addressed to physical barriers to the pursuit of individual ends. People with disabilities cannot be said to have equal opportunity as long as they are denied access to large areas of the physical environment. Sections 503 and 504 advance the concept of equal opportunity further: 504 ensures that disabled people have the same chance as other citizens to benefit from federally supported service programs, and 503 calls for an active effort to employ disadvantaged job-seekers. Despite the number of variations on equal opportunity, the Rehabilitation Act's conception of the citizen is more or less constant. Disabled citizens are, by virtue of their functional loss, incomplete; the state must compensate them so that they can participate in self-government. As one United States senator expressed it, "There should be no cost limits on helping handicapped individuals *to live free* in a democratic society" (emphasis added).

A desire for equal opportunity has in recent years motivated persons with amputations and other disabled people to form political organizations to advance their interests. The rehabilitation legislation of the 1970s was itself the result of political activity by such groups. The American Coalition of Citizens with Disabilities (ACCD) is the largest cross-disability citizens (as opposed to, say, veterans) coalition in the United States. Founded in 1974 by disability activist Frank Bowe, ACCD is an umbrella organization for other national groups, state coalitions (like the Massachusetts Coalition of Citizens with Disabilities), and individual state organizations such as Handicaps Unlimited of Virginia and New Jersey Disabled in Action. ACCD's voting members are groups that operate primarily for people with disabilities and at the direction of governing bodies with disabled majorities (interview with ACCD official).

Coalition-building among disability groups is difficult according to some activists (interviews). First, well-established disability-specific organizations may hesitate to risk hard-won benefits on an alliance with less powerful groups. Blind people, for example, have a long history of highly organized and successful political activity; coalition-building has little to offer them. Second, people with one disability are in many instances as ignorant of and uncomfortable with people with other disabilities as able-bodied people are. For this reason, ACCD devotes some of its resources to consciousness-raising among disabled people about the impairments, limitations, and capacities of others. Third, disability groups may oppose one another on substantive issues. It is to be expected, for example, that physical accessibility is less urgent for people with communication disabilities than for those with spinal-cord injuries. And conflicting philosophies of disability may divide potential allies. The long-standing dispute between oralists and manualists in the deaf community surely constrains political activity by this disability group. Sign-language interpretation is for one faction anathema and for the other a political goal and tool. Long-time disability activist Rita Varela reports two additional points of conflict: how radical a group is in its style and goals and whether it is tightly or loosely organized (Varela, 1983).

Frances Fox Piven and Richard Cloward point out that protest movements entail a change in consciousness as well as behavior (Piven and Cloward, 1977). The transformation as they see it has three aspects, and each seems to be present in the disability rights movement. First, the prevailing order loses legitimacy for those who protest. People with disabilities are calling into question policies made by able-bodied officials, policies that maintain a system in which disabled people are at a disadvantage. Some disabled people conceive of themselves explicitly as an oppressed minority. According to Piven and Cloward, these are likely to be people who have experienced discrimination in a concrete setting that in turn has provided opportunities for protest. The independent living movement is a good example. It began among severely disabled people in long-term care facilities, and deinstitutionalization, or "independent living," has become a focus for the disability rights movement in general. A second aspect is what Piven and Cloward identify as an end to fatalism among protesters. There is a belief among disability activists that the old order can be changed. Finally, there is a new sense of efficacy among people with disabilities. They publicly call attention to their abilities, and even severely disabled people are making use of residual capacities to be effective individually and in groups. Of course, disability activists, like other activists, can be found along a broad ideological spectrum. While some continue to work through traditional voluntary organizations like the March of Dimes, the Congress of the Physically Handicapped informs readers of its newspaper that "we receive no funds from the establishment, therefore the Bulletin is published and distributed with no fear of intimidation."

The conception of the citizen with an amputation as less than equal in a world of equals suggests that technological compensation has political ramifications. First, compensatory technology may in some instances achieve full restoration; it may create real functional equality. Political action by people with spinal-cord injuries has taken the motto "Cure Not Care" (interview with disability activist), and researchers at Wright State University claim that individuals with spinal-cord injuries will be able to walk with the help of computer-controlled electric current (*New York Times,* Nov. 12, 1982). If this breakthrough were to occur, the disabled community in general and the disability rights movement in particular would be greatly changed. Not every injury would prove reversible, and the return of some paraplegic persons to the able-bodied population would fractionate one of the most highly organized and articulate groups of disabled people. Furthermore, some activists hold that a development like the one foreseen at Wright State would stigmatize people who are not treatable—people with older or more severe injuries, for example—and weaken them politically (interview with disability activist).

Second, compensatory technology is only one response to functional loss. Assuming finite resources, equipment-embodied options are pursued at the expense of others, including monetary compensation and the protection of civil rights. Rehabilitation technology can be viewed in this context as an in-kind measure, and arguments for cash over in-kind benefits have been made in years of social policy debate. The point is especially well taken here, because most devices (including the Boston Elbow) provide less than perfect restoration, and cash benefits may be used to purchase a technology anyway. Furthermore, it may be that the legislative mandate to integrate disabled people "has done more to get technology available . . . than has any particular research or design project" (Fay, 1982, p. 44).

Third, technology is a service strategy in an era of rights. As a means of solving social problems, services have increasingly given way to legal redress, and although disability activists remain desirous of technological advance, they view it critically (interviews). According to some activists, technological responses to functional loss build false expectations of recovery and distract disabled people from coming to terms with impairment. The promise of a technological fix makes them impatient with the physical and social accommodations that must be made in the present. Similarly, the disability rights movement may lose activists to tomorrow's technique. If total reconstitution is at hand, people with disabilities may be less likely to organize in pursuit of common goals. And faith in technological solutions may turn attention from people and issues. To the extent that disabled people define themselves around machines, they have lost the real independence that the best compensatory technology offers.

Fourth, choices among compensatory technologies have a political aspect. The choice of "low" over "high" technology, for example, seems to affirm the user's autonomy; he or she understands the device and can maintain it. Disability activists also favor the fruits of "co-invention" (e.g., Kaplan, 1982, p. 91)—that is, of collaboration between engineer and user. One rehabilitation engineer advocates "grassroots technology," including "scrounging," which decentralizes innovation even if it does not democratize it. As for the danger that such an approach will violate existing arrangements for inventing and diffusing compensatory devices, he says, "There is, in fact, no system. There is just a patchwork of methods of getting technology into the hands and under the rears of disabled people" (Tobias, 1982, p. 103). Still, high technology has advantages too. Wearers of the Boston Elbow may give up "access," but they recover "innateness." In surrendering control over design and maintenance to specialists, the user regains natural physical control of his elbow.

Finally, the design and development of versatile technologies may create shared goals among disabled people. This is a point of contrast between person-focused measures and environmental ones. But even personal devices can be made more or less generalizable. Researchers at the Palo Alto Veterans Administration Hospital, for example, are working on robotic compensation for the loss of a limb: an arm-like manipulator is mounted near but not joined to the user. Engineers on the project claim that the manipulator has broader applicability than any prosthesis and keeps them out of "the historical rut of making expensive custom devices." In addition, because robotic arms have no pretensions to being body parts, the user "is more free to interact critically with the machine" (Swaine, 1983, p. 23). If a Palo Alto arm can be designed for general use, persons with amputations may find common cause with quadriplegic people as well as with one another in making the device available to those who can use it.

In summary, regardless of the way in which the citizen is defined, government is unlikely to offer him or her a Boston Elbow. Medicaid is welfare medicine. It provides only what is necessary and determines this in a context of reluctant and arguably inadequate funding. Federal research and regulation, designed to modulate the market, are indirect in their effect on the distribution of prostheses. And although the rehabilitation legislation of the 1970s represents a major improvement in the relationship between government and people with disabilities, it also emphasizes environmental as opposed to person-focused compensation. It is ironic that in order to secure equal opportunity for disabled people, public policy has diminished attention to the diffusion of compensatory technologies to individuals.

The dominant models of technological diffusion do not elucidate these limitations. They do not include alternatives like civil rights legislation, nor do they consider the appeal of this approach to disabled people and their advocates. The passage of the Rehabilitation Act and its amendments offers the citizen with an amputation new compensatory options that are related to the Boston Elbow in its ultimate goals but effective at a different level of intervention.

5
Policy-Holders
The Privately Insured

Discussion of the compensatory options of persons with amputations has to this point focused on public programs; government's response to disability is the subject of this study. Private compensation for functional loss, however, is an alternative for many people and may affect the scope of governmental responsibility. Although previous chapters have contrasted the public-sector arrays of veterans, workers, and citizens, none has specified the extent to which these policies diverge from what is available privately. The purpose of this chapter, then, is to sketch a backdrop of private responses to functional loss and to suggest how these options are different from those discussed in Chapters 2, 3, and 4. In fact, the market seems to face many of the same obstacles as government in diffusing the Boston Elbow.

The Privately Insured Person's Array

The compensatory options of the privately insured person with an amputation are depicted in Figure 9. These may include all but intervention in the social environment or comprise only the most limited medical care or income maintenance. This is an important distinction between public and private responses to functional loss: private

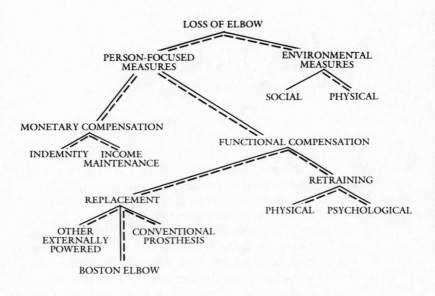

THE PRIVATE INSURANCE COMPENSATORY ARRAY
Figure 9

responses have greater within-group variation. Depending on the contractual language of a private insurance policy, the beneficiary may be covered for almost everything or for next to nothing. Contractual language, moreover, represents an explicit agreement between insurer and insured. The privately insured person knows exactly what he or she is insured for and agrees to these conditions.

With reference to the array, the policy-holder may first be entitled to modified housing or transportation. These may fall within his or her health or automobile liability coverage, although environmental modification is not actually specified in these policies and is undertaken at the discretion of the insurer. Alteration of the beneficiary's surroundings is likely to occur when this will allow for home as opposed to hospital care and when, consequently, total costs to the firm may be less. Admittedly, the person with an upper-extremity amputation does not frequently present the opportunity for this kind of savings. Persons with lower-extremity amputations and paraplegic persons, however, are often cared for more economically in a modified home environment (Mittelmann and Settele, 1982; interviews with for-profit insurance company officials). Blue Cross/Blue Shield does not pay for environmental modification (interviews with BC/BS Association staff and Massachusetts BC/BS official).

The private insurance policy-holder may receive monetary benefits, and these take the form of indemnity or income maintenance. In comparison with those paid in the public sector, private money benefits are of a staggering and highly specified variety. They break down roughly into three groups: those for employees, those for self-employed persons, and those unrelated to employment status. The privately insured person may be indemnified through his or her employer or union for the hospital costs of treating accidental dismemberment resulting from work. The same sort of benefit may be part of his life insurance policy, and hospital indemnities range from about $10 to $100 per day for some specified number of days. Accidental dismemberment itself is insured at some percentage of accidental death, which can mean a payment of $5,000 to $250,000. When a worker's disability is considered total and permanent and he or she is covered for group life insurance benefits, there may be an indefinite waiver of the life insurance premium in addition to fixed cash benefits received monthly over a period of months (HIAA, 1979; all citations to HIAA, 1979, are to pp. 28–37).

The privately insured worker may also be entitled to income maintenance payments, and employers and unions offer both long-term and short-term disability income insurance. Short-term income maintenance generally takes the form of a fixed weekly amount or a percentage of the worker's salary, say, 60 to 70 percent. Two hundred and fifty dollars is a common weekly maximum. Long-term benefits are paid in a similar manner, sometimes at a lower percentage of weekly income, and with a maximum of $3,000 per month. In order to qualify for short-term or long-term disability income, the worker must be unable to do his or her own job. Benefits of more than two years' duration require that he or she be unable to participate in any "suitable" occupation (HIAA, 1979).

Workers may receive private benefits contingent on termination owing to disability. Some are retirement plan benefits, either accrued benefits at the time of termination or deferred benefits at the regular retirement date. Another offering is profit-sharing or thrift arrangements. These may involve distribution of a lump sum or payment over the course of a lifetime (HIAA, 1979).

The person with an amputation who is self-employed or owns a business may also be entitled to cash benefits. Private policy-holders who cannot fulfill their job responsibilities can, through business overhead expense insurance, collect for business expenses incurred while they are disabled. The maximum payment is $8,000 per month, and the maximum duration of the benefit is about two years. Buy-sell disability income is also contingent on being unable to do one's job. It will pay up to 80 percent of fair market value of the disabled businessman's ownership interests; the benefit may take the form of a lump sum or of installment payments over one to five years (HIAA, 1979).

Private insurance policy-holders do not have to be workers to receive monetary compensation for their disability. They have several options. Hospital indemnity insurance may be purchased, as may accidental death and dismemberment insurance, although in both cases individual benefits may differ somewhat from the corresponding group (that is, employee) benefits. In the case of upper-extremity amputation, accidental dismemberment insurance can pay a policy-holder as much as $500,000. The non-worker may also insure himself or herself against travel accidents or buy coverage under general liability insurance for injury by another person. In addition to these indemnities, the privately insured person may receive income maintenance payments if he or she is unable to do his or her own work in the short run and any "suitable" work in the long run. The benefit is usually set at between $100 and $5,000 per month and held to 60 to 70 percent of an individual's gross income. Optional additions to the policy include increased compensation during hospitalization and a partial or residual disability rider (HIAA, 1979).

Private insurance for disability income is also available for injuries resulting from automobile accidents. In twenty-six states, no-fault automobile insurance is required of all drivers, and it commonly pays cash benefits with a weekly maximum of up to the beneficiary's actual income and usually with some aggregate maximum. Traditional automobile insurance offers income maintenance as an optional benefit at levels of $100 to $250 per week (HIAA, 1979).

The final item on this long list of money benefits is coverage of credit, mortgage, and life insurance payments. Both credit and mortgage disability payments are made to disabled policy-holders at first if they can no longer work at their own occupations and after two to five years if they cannot do any "suitable" work. Credit insurance benefits are available in the amount and for the duration of an individual's monthly loan payments, subject to a maximum of up to $15,000. Mortgage insurance usually covers the monthly loan payments for the term of the loan, subject to a maximum of $50,000. When an individual's disability is total and permanent, he or she may be granted a waiver of premium payments on his or her life insurance policy (HIAA, 1979).

Functional compensation also appears in the array of the privately insured person. Both retraining and replacement may be provided under group or individual health insurance policies or as settlement of an automobile liability claim. Private health insurance is purchased from a for-profit insurance company or under the non-

profit Blue Cross/Blue Shield plan. Health services are provided on a
fee-for-service basis or through a health maintenance organization.
Like the monetary benefits described above, private medical coverage may be narrow or comprehensive, and insurers offer a range of
plans.

The most comprehensive contracts offer physical rehabilitation
on an in-patient basis. Occupational therapy is not generally a covered service because it is not considered medical treatment. But
when occupational therapists provide basic rehabilitation for persons
with upper-extremity amputations, insurers define it as physical therapy and thus allowable, often with specific time limitations. Occupational therapy benefits may also be purchased on a rider. Replacement of the lost limb does not necessarily accompany retraining, and
the privately insured person may choose to learn to function without
a prosthesis. Some contracts also include the psychiatric benefits that
constitute psychological retraining after functional loss, but compensatory counseling here must have a distinctly medical cast. Workers'
compensation and the Vocational Rehabilitation Program, in contrast, use counseling as a source of information for the client or an
opportunity to assess his or her future "productivity." (Unless otherwise stated, this chapter's data about private health insurance were
collected from medical directors at two large for-profit insurance
companies and staff at several HMOs.)

Replacement frequently appears in group health insurance
plans, either in the basic benefits package or as a purchasable option.
Coverage decisions about prostheses are made at several levels. First
is the coverage provided in a particular contract. The most modest
benefit packages do not include prosthetic devices; even federally
qualified HMOs are not required to provide prostheses. When a
plan does offer artificial limbs, it may be at a fixed dollar amount or
with a co-payment by the policy-holder. In many cases, the Boston
Elbow and other costly devices are not excluded by the contractual
language, but neither for-profit nor non-profit insurers are likely to
process routinely a claim for a $5,000 elbow. At Massachusetts
Blue Cross/Blue Shield (which was described by a national BC/BS
staffer interviewed for this study as the most medically sophisticated), the claims processor would probably refer the request for

such an uncommon and expensive device to his or her supervisor. The supervisor might rule—on the basis of previous decisions or an understanding of the plan's overall policy—or the claim might be reviewed at successively higher levels until it reached the Medical Advisory Committee. This group consists of thirty-eight physicians who chair specialty sub-committees and it deliberates on whether a procedure or device is medically necessary, whether it is in general use, and whether it is of demonstrated value. There is also a less well-articulated concern with alternatives and their costs. Contracts sometimes call for the least expensive alternative, but even where a plan is mute, cost is increasingly a problem for Blue Cross/Blue Shield administrators and their advisors. Finally, the organization is sensitive to public opinion (interview with BC/BS official).

According to Liberty Mutual officials, a claim for a Boston Elbow has been submitted to Blue Cross/Blue Shield of Massachusetts, which has not yet notified Liberty Mutual of its decision. Whatever it is, the ruling will apply only in Massachusetts. Coverage policy is made by each carrier, and there may be significant regional variation in reimbursement policy regarding the Boston Elbow. In plans where decision-makers are uncertain about what course to take, they may request assistance from the national BC/BS Association. A staff member there, who had been asked to review a claim for a myoelectric hand prosthesis, said he would try to answer the following questions: Is the amputation bi-lateral? Is the recipient physically incapable of using the conventional alternative? Is the marginal benefit equal to the marginal cost? Is the documentation of patient need sufficient to support expenditure of such a large sum? Is this a device for which there are likely to be many claims? At least as Blue Cross/Blue Shield views the Boston Elbow, the relatively small number of persons with above-elbow amputations may work to the advantage of the claimants (interview).

Other private insurers review unusual claims for prostheses in much the same way. Claims processors alert their supervisors, who have access to a staff of medical specialists within the organization. Again, a contract that covers limb prostheses will not distinguish among them, and devices like the Boston Elbow are therefore not excluded by contractual language. (In fact, Motion Control reports [written communication] that as many as ten for-profit insurers have approved claims for the Utah Arm.) Rather, medical officials reviewing a case will consider whether a device is medically necessary and whether it is in general use. Doctors in two insurance firms and several HMO staff explained that they rely heavily on the prescribing physician to demonstrate that a prosthesis matches the needs of a particular patient. The medical literature, professional societies, and organizations associated with specific diseases may provide additional data.

Like Blue Cross/Blue Shield, for-profit insurers express a desire to avoid an unflattering public image. One firm is promoting "medical management" of claims—that is, a kind of ongoing consultation that softens the adversarial relationship between insurer and insured by resolving coverage questions before the patient purchases or sets his or her heart on a device. Prescribing physicians, patients, and claims processors are encouraged to discuss the case among themselves and with officials at the home office. An official at another firm said he hoped to avoid a public debate about what is legitimate emergency room care by reimbursing whatever services emergency rooms are willing to provide (interviews). In contrast with Blue Cross/Blue Shield, other insurers talked less about cost and more about making good medical judgments (interviews). This may be a matter of style or public relations, but there is also an economic reason for the difference. Blue Cross/Blue Shield sells only one product—health insurance—while for-profit firms typically sell life, automobile, and workers' compensation insurance as well. The for-profit insurers are therefore able to make up on other kinds of policies anything they lose on a claim for a medical technology. In fact, the insurance industry first marketed health insurance as a way to lure clients into buying the more profitable life insurance (Hetherington et al., 1975).

Insurers expressed interest in retaining control over the distribution of unusual and costly benefits like the Boston Elbow. The device will be provided, if at all, on a case-by-case basis, and the characteristics of the prospective wearer will figure prominently in the decision. It seems important that the client be young and active and that he or she live near a maintenance facility. One official said he would look for evidence of sufficient intellect to use the device—this despite the fact that myoelectric prostheses are designed to be easier to use. Those who distribute expensive technologies seemed to favor appreciative recipients. One insurer suggested that the myoelectric prostheses be "a little harder to get." This way, only a strongly motivated policy-holder would receive one.

In the private sector, functional compensation is not related to monetary benefits. Non-profit insurers have no responsibility for monetary compensations, and although many for-profit health insurers also pay disability income benefits, the two kinds of policies are administered independently. A holder of firm A's health insurance policy may well receive his disability income payments from firm B, although one of the firms contacted for this study is considering rehabilitation benefits for disability income beneficiaries. According to a company official, a rehabilitation counselor will be employed to identify potential rehabilitants and offer them functional compensation. The firm plans not to formalize this option by writing it into disability income contracts and expects to offer rehabilitation benefits only to the most promising policy-holders and those who are insured for sizeable sums in income maintenance.

Private Insurance and the Boston Elbow

In general, privately insured persons with amputations may receive Boston Elbows if their coverage extends to prosthetics and their physicians can convince their insurers that the device is appropriate for them. Private sector insurers do set broad limits as to what is health technology and what is not, and they eschew what some insurance officials call "Cadillacs" and "convenience items." One insurance company, for example, rejected a claim for a waterproof lower-extremity prosthesis (the so-called "swimming leg" provided to veterans with service-connected amputations) because the firm considers "fitness" beyond the responsibility of the health insurer. It also refused to pay for a bathroom scale for a patient who had to lose weight for medical reasons. Another firm approved an air conditioner for a policy-holder with pulmonary disease but only for one room of his house. But, when interviewed, the medical directors of these firms viewed the Boston Elbow as neither a Cadillac nor a convenience item. They recognized that the device replaces a missing body part and that its increased cost buys enhanced functioning. One Boston-area HMO, on the other hand, declines to cover myoelectric limbs because they are not yet "customary."

For the private sector, rehabilitation is a coverage area that is hard to define. Complete rehabilitation, or "maximum rehabilitation," as one BC/BS staffer put it, may not be a health insurer's responsibility. Vocational rehabilitation, for example, is not covered under any group health insurance policy. Still, almost any rehabilitation technology will fall short of the human capacity it is meant to replace, so the insurer is always providing a less than "maximal" device. One insurance company official asserted that upper-extremity devices are "tools" at best, that without sensation, no prosthesis can replace a limb, that even a Boston Elbow will never be the dominant arm of a person with a unilateral amputation. In a case like this the health insurer must determine when a technology provides enough rehabilitation to be effectual but no more rehabilitation than is medically—as opposed to vocationally or recreationally—indicated.

A salient difference between private insurance and public programs is that the private sector operates by the rules of the market. Both the for-profit and non-profit insurers identify the person with an amputation primarily as a consumer. He or she pays, directly or indirectly, for his or her health insurance coverage, choosing among multiple, varied combinations of benefits. Unlike Medicaid recipients, private insurance policy-holders can buy more or less care. Unlike Medicare beneficiaries, they can negotiate for more coverage at the same price. Their relationship with their insurers is that of buyers with sellers, of equals engaged in a transaction in the interest of both. Private insurers may sell as much or as little coverage as they want to provide; buyers have the option of finding other sellers. Public programs, in contrast, represent public purposes, and potential beneficiaries are often required to participate. In the public sector, the relationship between insurer and insured is also that of governor and governed. It is a relationship shaped, not by the threat of taking one's business elsewhere, but through the complex give-and-take of the political process.

Politics are more influential in non-profit than in for-profit private health plans. When asked to distinguish his organization from for-profit insurance firms, a Blue Cross/Blue Shield official rolled his eyes and said "regulation." He added that he has a mandate to serve the people and that this means living with the vicissitudes of state politics. Blue Cross/Blue Shield is, however, only "pseudopublic," in his words. Politics affects its operation but not so "abruptly" as in the truly public sector (interview). While for-profit insurers are accountable only to their stockholders, public programs, and to a lesser extent Blue Cross/Blue Shield, are accountable to the polity. Similarly, equity is a ground rule, however obscured, in the public sector. In any case, private insurance policy-holders use a different currency of exchange than do veterans, workers, or citizens. The former may secure a Boston Elbow by shopping for the most generous policy; the latter transact business with ballots, lobbies, and other forms of political activity.

Private health insurers sometimes respond to the offerings of their public counterparts. Insurance company officials interviewed for this study cited Medicare as having framed their concept of "medical necessity," for example. Furthermore, many private health insurance policies provide only what Medicare does not—that is, policy-holders are covered for the expenses they incur in excess of their Medicare benefits. At least one private insurer uses Medicare reimbursement policy to justify exclusion of particular procedures and devices. Claimants are told, "If the government won't cover it . . . " (interviews).

As for the Boston Elbow, it may well be provided to the privately insured person with an amputation. For-profit insurers seem not to hesitate as much as public payers in providing such a device, at least in providing the Utah Arm (written communication from Motion Control). But in interviews with officials of two other insurance companies, references to the Liberty Mutual Insurance Company were acerbic. Both firms sell workers' compensation as well as group health insurance, and they compete with Liberty Mutual for clients.

Their officials admitted that Liberty enjoys a public reputation for rehabilitation-mindedness, but they attributed the image to Liberty's "selling job" rather than its track record. Workers' compensation insurers who refuse to buy the Boston Elbow, may be less reluctant to buy an expensive arm prosthesis than to fill the coffers of a competitor.

The compensatory array of the privately insured person diverges from those of the veteran, worker, and citizen, especially in its underlying principles. There are, however, significant similarities between private and public arrays. First, the private sector is no more orderly than the public sector. There may be several government agencies mandated to deal with disability, but there are at least as many insurers, and it is possible to buy one sort of policy from one and another sort of policy from another. There may be many public programs that respond to functional loss, but there are at least as many kinds of health and disability income insurance. A health insurance policy can be written to reflect the preferences of every client, and members of client groups often have several plans from which to choose. Disability income, as described above, is distributed in myriad ways, sometimes for very specific purposes. Coordination is no likelier to occur in the private sector than in the public, although a "market basket" of private insurance may be ideologically less offensive than the bureaucratic disarray of unrelated public policies. The private insurance policy-holder must in any event choose among many options from many sources.

A second similarity between private and public arrays is that those who design and administer them are more or less dependent on medical expertise. Both private insurers and public programs employ and consult with physicians and in some cases prosthetists, physical therapists, and rehabilitation specialists. In both sectors, the client's physician initiates and sustains the request for compensatory technology. The doctor must justify a device's cost, and his or her effectiveness as an advocate may determine the outcome of the claim.

Finally, private and public arrays represent situations in which specific policies are applied to specific cases through a loosely defined and discretionary process (Greenberg and Derzon, 1981). Like the public programs described in Chapters 2, 3, and 4, Blue Cross/

Blue Shield and the for-profit insurers draw broad distinctions between reimbursable and non-reimbursable items but leave the interpretation of these general rules to the individuals who review specific claims. Some directives regarding compensatory technologies originate in the private sector, but it would be a mistake to think that the future of the Boston Elbow will be decided in a definitive way either there or in the public sector. Not only is the Boston Elbow too uncommon a request to compete for the attention of top-level policymakers, but as an aid to functioning rather than a health technology *per se,* the device will likely be distributed selectively to individuals who demonstrate the capacity and inclination to use it well.

6
Conclusions
Good Laws and Good Arms

The chief foundations of all states . . . are good laws and good arms.
—Machiavelli

It has been the intention of this research essay to depict government's diffusion of compensatory technology and to argue that these devices are one means to the ends of disability policy—the redistribution of functional loss. Acts of God and man create disability, but public policy determines how the compensatory burden will fall. Chapters 2, 3, and 4 above describe the compensation to which veterans, workers, and citizens with amputations are entitled. In some cases, it includes a sophisticated elbow prosthesis known as the Boston Elbow.

This study departs from earlier diffusion research in that it uses a contextual framework to organize inquiry. Figure 2, when applied to government's diffusion of the Boston Elbow, sets the device among other responses to loss of an arm and reveals the different strategies by which different classes of people with amputations are compensated. The first part of this chapter reviews the compensatory arrays described in preceding chapters and defines the principles on which they operate. It then modestly extends contextual analysis to other health technologies.

The role of technology in disability policy is subtle and complex. Most obviously, devices assume human functions that have been lost: the Boston Elbow, for example, restores the ability to lift, hold, and position objects. Technology also shapes relationships between disabled and able-bodied people. Wheelchairs without push handles do not invite assistance. Machines are tools of social policy. They may serve disparate purposes, and often the same device is employed to more than one end. Still, even technologies with many uses incline the user toward some kinds of activity over others. Adapted telephones, for example, can be used for checking on mother or playing the horses, but they always incline the user toward increased interaction. Technologies are sometimes built to carry out particular compensatory strategies. The Boston Elbow, for example, was designed to promote functional over monetary compensation. Some artifacts come to serve a strategy long after they are designed: institutions built decades earlier became a means of organizing disabled people for independent living in the 1970s.

Technology is an agent of disability policy—of the public redistribution of functional loss. But devices also become distributive mechanisms in their own right. As Winner suggests, artifacts not only serve policy but make it. They often perpetuate the redistribution they were enlisted to serve, although they may undermine it. Sometimes they redefine the disability they were meant to mitigate. The last part of this chapter explores the ways in which government's decision to deploy a device is really only a first stage in technological policy-making.

Good Laws

For government, people with above-elbow amputations are veterans, workers, and citizens. Preceding chapters have mapped each group's compensatory options. Table 2 summarizes this information by displaying all significant subgroups against all significant options; the Boston Elbow appears, but not in every program. This study has understood the diffusion of compensatory technology as representa-

Table 2. SUMMARY OF PUBLIC PROGRAMS

PROGRAMS	ENVIRONMENTAL		MONETARY		FUNCTIONAL		REPLACEMENT		MAJOR PRINCIPLES
	Social	Physical	Indemnity	Income Maintenance	Replace	Retrain	Boston Elbow	Other	
VETERANS									
Service-connected	X	X	(combined)		X	X		X	to provide everything possible to recognize veteran
Non-service-connected	X			X	X	X		X	similar to but less generous than above
WORKERS									
Workers' Compensation		X	X	X	X	X	X	X	to pay for loss, return worker to work
SSDI/Medicare				X	X	X		X	to provide social wage
VR Program	X	X			X	X	X	X	to allow realization of potential for work
CITIZENS									
SSI/Medicaid				X	X	X		X	to maintain
Research and regulation	X								to subsidize and police devices
Rehabilitation Act and amendments	X	X							to ensure equal opportunity

tive of larger policy designs. Table 2, therefore, summarizes both compensatory measures and underlying principles. These principles articulate consistencies within programs and testify to the fact that public policy is not always arbitrary. Rather the policies that are the subject of this book derive logically and normatively from the ways in which government defines its constituencies.

The Veteran

The veteran has the largest number of compensatory options (see Figure 3). Veterans with service-connected amputations, in fact, are entitled to some form of every option, and, like veterans with non-service-connected amputations, are finally eligible for the Boston Elbow. As noted above, the VA's extended disinterest in the Boston Elbow resulted in part from a long-standing commitment to the VA Elbow. Newly powerful veterans system officials, however, are skeptical of the VA Elbow's usefulness and have approved not only the Boston Elbow but the Utah Arm and the NYU-Hosmer Elbow as well. Even now, however, VA clinic teams may favor the VA Elbow, since it is the device with which they are familiar and it can be serviced within the VA.

Another reason for the VA's lack of interest in the Boston Elbow is that, regardless of what prosthesis the veteran wears, he or she is also eligible for environmental modification, monetary compensation, and retraining. VA officials interviewed for this study were explicit about their goal—to do everything possible for the veteran with a service-connected disability. Prosthetics is only one compensatory measure, and hardware is arguably less desirable than its alternatives. Retraining may be preferable; occupational therapy enables most people with amputations to function adequately without a prosthesis. Modification of the social environment, the labor market, for example, may produce cash benefits that are in turn negotiable for functional compensation. The same is of course true of monetary compensation, another feature of the veteran's array. Cash appears to dominate the agendas of advocacy groups like Disabled American Veterans. Money, after all, is more reliable than hardware and compensates for any number of disabling conditions. The Boston Elbow, in contrast, is only one of several devices for a single disability, and experts do not agree about its ultimate usefulness.

This reading of the veterans system is admittedly ironic. The Veterans Administration has supported prosthetics research and development both at the VA and elsewhere, and the veteran with an amputation does receive relatively generous prosthetic services. Still, the veterans system is a system of *benefits*. The purpose of the compensatory array is to respond to the veteran's sacrifice in every possible way. If he or she wishes to work, he or she is helped to do so, but employment is not in itself a goal of the system. Benefits do not issue from an insurance policy, nor are they the concessions of a welfare state. Rather the disabled veteran is viewed as having a legitimate claim on whatever government can provide. Benefits include existing compensatory technologies and research on better ones, but they also take the form of affirmative action, disability compensation, occupational therapy, and other programs. Elbow prostheses mitigate loss, and the Boston Elbow is a fine prosthesis. But the veterans system will diffuse the device as one benefit among many, and on these terms the Boston Elbow may not diffuse to every veteran with an above-elbow amputation.

The Worker

The compensatory array of the worker with an amputation is actually three sets of options. First, the individual who loses an arm in the workplace receives workers' compensation benefits that usually comprise monetary and functional measures (see Figure 4). In most states, the program both indemnifies the worker's physical integrity and replaces lost wages with income maintenance until the beneficiary earns at least what he or she earned at the time of the amputation. It is thus in the interest of the workers' compensation insurer to restore as much of the beneficiary's work-related functioning as possible. The Liberty Mutual Insurance Company pursued this interest technologically. The Boston Elbow was designed to lessen income maintenance payments to persons with above-elbow amputations and to attract clients—that is, employers—whose experience-rated premiums would fall with the amount paid in income maintenance benefits.

The workers' compensation array is focused on the person, and unlike the veteran's array, it is held together not by prerogative but by terms of agreement among contending parties. Workers' compensation insurance protects both the worker from loss of work-related function and the employer from consequent legal action by the worker. An indemnity is paid when an employee sustains a loss in the workplace, and income maintenance payments accrue to the disabled employee until he or she returns to work. There is tension in this array: functional compensation, by restoring the worker's capacity for work, minimizes monetary compensation, and workers' compensation beneficiaries thus have an economic incentive not to be rehabilitated. Still, income maintenance is always a lesser sum than wages, and disability often necessitates additional expenditures. Furthermore, at least in Massachusetts, the Industrial Accidents Board (IAB) takes a dim view of workers' compensation clients who refuse retraining or replacement so as to avoid returning to work. These beneficiaries violate the terms of the workers' compensation agreement, and while the IAB may press an insurer for increased rehabilitation services, the worker is also required to participate fully in the rehabilitation process. A prosthesis is in this context a *tool* provided by the insurer to re-equip the disabled worker for work. Competition among insurers, though, may inhibit the diffusion of Liberty Mutual's Elbow to the workers' compensation beneficiaries of other firms.

Some workers are beneficiaries of Social Security Disability Insurance (SSDI). Totally disabled individuals who have participated in the Social Security system and whose disabilities are expected to last at least twelve months receive income maintenance payments based on past wages. After two years as an SSDI recipient, he or she is also eligible for Medicare benefits (see Figure 5). SSDI, like workers' compensation, is an insurance program, but SSDI collects premiums from both the worker and the employer, and the disability against which workers are insured does not have to result from activities in the workplace. The Boston Elbow is unlikely to appear in the SSDI array. The device could be provided through Medicare but has not yet been approved by program officials. And even if the device is approved, Medicare will not provide it until the worker has spent two years in the SSDI program—virtually until he or she has adjusted to amputation without it.

The Social Security Disability Insurance array is focused on the person and not the environment. It is less generous than the veteran's array, consisting exclusively of one form of monetary compensation and the delayed retraining and replacement that Medicare offers. These rehabilitation services are not intended to minimize income maintenance payments. SSDI beneficiaries who are considered potentially re-employable are referred to another program, the federal/state Vocational Rehabilitation (VR) Program, whose charge is to keep the SSDI rolls as short as possible. Medicare provides only "medically necessary" prostheses and rehabilitation. It is designed to maintain former workers with total and long-term disabilities, not to transform disabled workers into able-bodied ones. The two-year lag in Medicare benefits underscores this point. SSDI recipients, who are by definition workers, may have private health insurance in the early stages of their disability; in any case, Medicare benefits do not begin for twenty-four months. Thus even if Medicare provides a Boston Elbow, it will not do so immediately after amputation, and this is when the potential user draws up his or her compensatory strategy. It is worth noting in this regard that the two-year Medicare lag has different effects on different kinds of disabilities. Medical coverage of degenerative conditions begins in the later, more debilitating, stages. Stable disabilities, like amputation, however, are most serious at onset, when Medicare coverage is not available.

The worker's third set of compensatory options is provided by the federal/state Vocational Rehabilitation Program. Persons whose disabilities are both an obstacle to employment and remediable by VR services are entitled under the program to those compensatory measures that will increase their employability. The VR client is the potential worker, and as noted in Figure 6, the VR array comprises environmental modification and functional compensation, including the Boston Elbow. Cash beneficiaries through SSDI and Supplemental Security Income (SSI) are referred to the VR Program if they are judged to have employment potential. The Vocational Rehabilitation Program is funded through federal and state revenues and is expected to realize public savings by enabling disabled workers to work.

The VR array is both environmental and person-focused. Unlike workers' compensation insurance, VR provides cumulative, not competing, benefits. Unlike SSDI, VR does not so much serve workers as create them. The range of Vocational Rehabilitation services is broad, including prostheses, physical and occupational therapy, job training and vocational education, and modified living and working environments, but these options are not held together by an ethos, like the VA's, of doing everything possible for the client. Rather, like workers' compensation insurance, the VR Program revolves around employability and, in the case of SSI and SSDI beneficiaries, sustains a tension between monetary and functional compensation. Unlike workers' compensation, Vocational Rehabilitation does not represent an explicit bargain among worker, employer, and insurer. The VR counselor sets the terms of a client's participation and enjoys considerable discretion in both the admissions process and subsequent service planning. Furthermore, whereas virtually every individual injured in the workplace is a workers' compensation beneficiary, the VR Program chooses among potential clients. Until passage of the Rehabilitation Act of 1973, counselors consistently admitted less seriously disabled people in order to maximize the number of job placements. Counselors are now required to serve people with severe disabilities first, but the program is still judged by the number of clients who find and keep jobs. Under these conditions, VR officials are sometimes moved to purchase Boston Elbows. The program provides compensation for the purpose of realizing vocational potential. Here, as in the workers' compensation array, prosthetics is a *tool* with which the potential worker makes his way into the labor force.

The Citizen

The compensatory array of the citizen with an amputation offers both subsistence and basic medical care for low-income persons (see Figure 7) and a convergence of environmental measures, physical and social (see Figure 8). Eligibility criteria for the amputee-citizen's options are less stringent than those for veterans or workers. In fact, every person with an amputation is a citizen with an amputation, and apart from means-testing for Supplemental Security Income and Medicaid, the citizen's array is accessible to all. It does not include the Boston Elbow, which is a person-focused option whose cost commonly exceeds the fiscal constraints of the welfare system.

The citizen's compensatory array has changed considerably since the early 1970s. In 1972, the federal Supplemental Security Income program replaced spotty state welfare benefits for old people and people with disabilities. SSI was linked to Medicaid, and states were given the option to provide prostheses and other rehabilitation services to SSI recipients. SSI resembles SSDI in that beneficiaries must be totally disabled and expected to remain so for at least twelve months. SSI benefits, however, are computed exclusively on the basis of financial need, and eligibility for Medicaid begins as soon as an individual is added to the SSI rolls. Like SSDI recipients, SSI clients who have employment potential are referred to the federal/state Vocational Rehabilitation Program. They may be provided with a Boston Elbow there but will receive only a "medically necessary" prosthesis from the Medicaid program. With the possible exception of very high amputations, loss of an arm does not make the Boston Elbow "medically necessary."

The Rehabilitation Act of 1973 introduced a *civil rights* strategy for compensating people for functional loss. These environmental measures rendered the disabled citizen's world easier to live in. Discrimination was outlawed in businesses and programs receiving federal support, and structures built with federal funds were required to be physically accessible. The 1978 amendments to this legislation advanced the environmental strategy further; they established independent living centers (ILCs), where people with severe disabilities could be helped in modifying their immediate environments. Environmental compensation had a strong normative aspect. While earlier rehabilitation service programs had defined disability as a personal inadequacy, the new measures assumed that society was inaccessible and that accessibility was a right. The Boston Elbow might be considered an aid to access, and the ILC legislation would in this case allow for the use of program funds to purchase the device. Public funding for the centers has been erratic, however, and only an ILC with exceptional private resources would be likely to allocate so much of its funding to a single device.

The National Institute of Handicapped Research was created in

1978 to take primary federal responsibility for disability research. The agency's mandate has always been greater than its resources, but its distribution of research and development funds constitutes one of the disabled citizen's compensatory options. Similarly, the Medical Devices Amendments of 1976 provided a means for the Food and Drug Administration to protect citizens with disabilities from unsafe and ineffective compensatory technologies. The market for prosthetics is one environment in which the citizen with an amputation finds himself. NIHR and the FDA stimulate and police the market respectively.

Other Laws and Other Arms

This essay uses the Boston Elbow to probe government's diffusion of compensatory technology. The kind of analysis done here, however, should generalize to other laws and other arms. What can be learned by stretching additional technologies over the contextual framework displayed in Figure 2? Amid what alternatives are these devices diffused? To which users through which public policies? According to what larger distributive principles? Three brief examples will indicate the usefulness of contextual analysis in studying other health technologies.

The M.I.T. Knee, like the Boston Elbow, is a cybernetic limb prosthesis. In 1985 it was not yet available commercially, although it was worn by research subjects in the laboratory. Public diffusion of the M.I.T. Knee will likely resemble that of the Boston Elbow. Both are sophisticated technologies for which there will always be less costly prosthetic and non-prosthetic alternatives. And policy for the Knee will be made separately for veterans, workers' compensation beneficiaries, Medicare and Medicaid recipients, and participants in the Vocational Rehabilitation Program.

There are significant differences, however, between the Boston Elbow and the M.I.T. Knee. Persons with lower-extremity amputations are more numerous than those with upper-extremity amputations. They are, as a whole, older, more often female, and more likely to lose a limb from systemic illness. Policies to redress the loss of a leg, then, will affect a larger number of people and may demand larger expenditures of public funds. Because trauma is less frequently the cause of lower- than upper-extremity amputation, workers' compensation insurers will be less influential in diffusing the M.I.T. Knee than they have been in diffusing the Boston Elbow. Medicare, in contrast, will be more influential because many lower-extremity amputations occur after age sixty-five, and elderly people are entitled to prosthetic benefits immediately upon amputation. Similarly, concern about incentives and disincentives to employment will play a lesser role. Potential Knee users will be generally less healthy; this may tilt the cost-benefit ratio away from diffusion.

Another significant difference between the Boston Elbow and the M.I.T. Knee is the desirability of one of the Knee's hardware alternatives: the wheelchair. Wheelchairs, body-powered and electric, serve not only people with amputations but those with spinal-cord injuries and neurological disorders such as multiple sclerosis and cerebral palsy. Wheelchairs are familiar and easy for physicians and bureaucrats to deal with. Wheelchairs are not, of course, a perfect alternative to the M.I.T. Knee. Users complain about the chair manufactured by the nearly monopolistic Everest and Jennings, and wheelchairs require ramps and curb cuts and modified transport. Consumers are only beginning to see improvements in chair design and the accessibility of the built environment. Still, the need for modification of public space has contributed to a wheelchair "movement," where people with amputations may find support and through which they may organize on other disability issues.

The choice between wheelchair and M.I.T. Knee raises issues encountered previously in this study. For example, how important is it to replace a missing body part with a device resembling the human anatomy? The wheelchair does not reproduce the lower extremities and is therefore more conspicuous than a good prosthesis. Similarly, which lost functions are most sorely missed, by persons with amputations and by the public programs that compensate them? Wheelchairs allow users to travel quickly but not to climb stairs. Which function has greater vocational significance, and will the workers' compensation and Vocational Rehabilitation programs restore this function rather than others? The VA may not readily approve the M.I.T. Knee owing to its origins outside the veterans system. The M.I.T. Knee may be favored generally because it alters the disabled person while the wheelchair alters the common space. These questions and possibilities are among those framed by Figure 2. Additional data and contextual analysis could be brought to bear for a complete understanding of public diffusion of the M.I.T. Knee.

The contextual framework may also be applied to psychotropic drugs, drugs prescribed to alter the user's mood or mental processes. Physicians commonly prescribe one group of psychotropics, the neuroleptics or "major tranquilizers," in treating psychosis, and these medications are thought to have "revolutionized" psychiatry. They manage the symptoms of many patients well enough to obviate the need for physical restraints and close supervision. They frequently make deinstitutionalization possible. In the terms of this study, psychotropic drugs are a compensatory technology. Few psychiatrists would claim that these substances "cure" psychosis or mood disorders. They seem instead to mitigate the effects. The neuroleptics are often prescribed for lengthy periods, during which they compensate in an ongoing way for the emotional and intellectual losses that occur with mental illness.

The contextual framework reveals the complexity of policy-making for psychotropic drugs. Pharmacology would appear in Figure 2 as one of several divergent treatment philosophies. These disparate measures reflect uncertainty about the nature of psychiatric disability, a set of illnesses about whose etiology, implications for functioning, and preferred forms of treatment experts disagree.

Psychotropic drugs are a person-focused technology, but environmental measures are also prominent in the treatment of mental illness. The most obvious of these is institutionalization—the asylum, a complete modification of the patient's physical and social environments. In the last century, mental hospitals were designed to create external order for people whose internal lives were considered dangerously disordered. More recently, milieu therapy has cultivated the compensatory potential of an institution's social relations. The community mental health movement exchanged one environmental strategy for another; it has drawn people out of institutions to surround them with a supportive normalcy.

Psychotropic drugs are one person-focused option, "replacement" in the terms of Figure 2. People with psychiatric disabilities may also be eligible for money benefits under a number of programs including SSDI and SSI. As with amputation, monetary compensation mitigates the employment-related losses of mental illness, and cash may be used to purchase other options. The most highly developed response to mental illness is psychotherapy, in the form of insight therapy, behavior modification, cognitive therapy, psychoanalysis, and so on. These would appear in the framework as "retraining, social" and are sometimes administered in combination with psychotropic drugs.

In the case of the Boston Elbow, public programs provide different classes of people with different compensatory strategies; to these discriminatory policies is sometimes attributed the modest rate at which the Elbow has diffused. Psychotropic drugs, in contrast, have diffused rapidly despite differences in entitlements among potential users. The pharmaceutical industry has promoted the drugs vigorously. And psychiatrists are apparently eager for pharmacological assistance. Moreover, psychotropics are not more expensive than their alternatives. The neuroleptics in fact produce a savings when they shorten hospitalization or the course of out-patient psychotherapy. Psychotropic drugs also benefit from their resemblance to other pharmaceuticals. Drug therapy is part of medical practice, and these drugs are easily integrated.

The contextual approach to the diffusion of technology emphasizes the behavior of public providers. A full analysis of psychotropic drugs would turn up many significant behaviors of this kind, and one would surely be the shift in responsibility for mental health care from the states to the federal government in the 1960s and 1970s. It is impossible to know precisely the role of psychotropic drugs in deinstitutionalization; the release of patients from mental hospitals is a complex phenomenon. It is certain, however, that the introduction of these medications coincided with the first waves of what was to be the exodus of hundreds of thousands of patients from psychiatric institutions. These were primarily state hospitals, and deinstitutionalization substantially reduced the contribution of state governments to mental health care. Federal programs, in turn, became increasingly important for the deinstitutionalized population, first by default and then with the expansion of entitlements to include SSI and Medicaid benefits. Psychotropic drugs continue to diffuse, and they continue to maintain large numbers of psychiatric patients in the community. Because it attends to competing sources of compensation, the contextual framework suggests a role even for a relationship like federalism in the diffusion of compensatory technologies.

A third application of the framework in Figure 2 is to the diaphragm, a contraceptive technology. Like the Boston Elbow, the diaphragm is a device, but its purpose is not to compensate for functional loss. Rather, the diaphragm takes the contextual framework beyond compensation to family planning—another health-related end to which there are many technological and non-technological means. The diaphragm is no longer an innovation, but technologies diffuse as long as humans use them, and changing circumstances may change patterns of diffusion. Even now, setting the diaphragm among its alternatives in different ways for different classes of users will reveal something about family planning policy.

In Figure 2, the first distinction among alternatives is whether a measure is person-focused or environmental. The only real environmental alternative to the diaphragm is the physical segregation of men and women. This is a drastic and impractical measure, although it is sometimes still imposed. Adoption is also arguably an environmental approach to family planning; it alters the environment to accomodate the "unplanned" child. Not surprisingly, adoption is favored by opponents of abortion, who condemn the person-focused, that is, the woman-focused, nature of that family planning strategy.

The diaphragm would appear in the contextual framework as person-focused hardware. Monetary measures are only relevant as incentives to other strategies, and governments sometimes employ cash benefits to increase or decrease birth rates. Other functional measures represent closer alternatives to the diaphragm: family planning "software" includes abstinence, withdrawal, and rhythm. Public policy is implicated in the use of these measures only to the extent that it frustrates use of more reliable hardware. Otherwise these activities elude governmental involvement. Unlike software alternatives to the Boston Elbow (for example, psychological counseling), abstinence, withdrawal, and rhythm are practiced without the participation of a regulatable professional. Unlike contraceptive hardware (for example, the condom), abstinence, withdrawal, and rhythm are not embodied in a regulatable good.

Family planning policy most often concerns itself with hard technologies that prevent conception or terminate pregnancy. These seem to fall into three policy-relevant groups: measures that act primarily on the woman, those that act primarily on the man, and those that act primarily on the fertilized ovum. The diaphragm falls into the first group, along with the pill, foam, and female sterilization. Condoms and male sterilization are to be found in the second group, and abortion and the IUD in the third. Depending on the group into which a technology falls, public policy regarding its use will be more or less complicated. In every case there is an artifact and consequently public laws and practices relating to its manufacture and sale. The woman too is always implicated in family planning; technologies that act on the man or the embryo necessarily act on the woman as well, and this may produce fundamental conflicts of interest for public policy to resolve. And even when the woman is the primary target of a contraceptive technology, successful use of the device may require the cooperation of her physician and her partner. This is true, for example, of the diaphragm, which should be inserted shortly before intercourse and is sized and prescribed for her. By organizing the collaborative act that is family planning in a specific way, the diaphragm creates relationships that are different from those created by abortion or abstinence. Such relationships are the locus and legacy of technological policy-making.

Figure 2 raises many questions about the diaphragm. How is the user of family planning technology viewed by government—by the veterans system or the Medicaid program? What combinations of family planning measures typify the welfare system and the private sector, and what distributional principles operate? How are controversies about effectiveness resolved? How is entitlement negotiated? What are the cost considerations for public programs, for users of contraception? What does contraceptive technology share with technologies that increase fertility? Are their patterns of diffusion similar? Answers to questions like these would surely contribute to depicting public diffusion of the diaphragm in its complexity.

Good Arms

The Boston Elbow is a sophisticated prosthetic technology. It is so innate as to tap residual biceps and triceps muscles to control flexion and extension of an artificial elbow joint. The Elbow is not highly accessible. It requires expert maintenance, and although it may be easy to use, its workings are not easily understood. The Boston Elbow differs from other elbow prostheses in several respects. It was designed to improve on body-powered devices, which are unattractive and inefficient to operate and do not allow for simultaneous use of elbow and hook or hand. The Boston Elbow, rather, runs on batteries, as do externally powered prostheses like the switch-controlled VA and NYU-Hosmer Elbows and the myoelectric Utah Arm. But switch-controlled devices are not proportional; they run at a single speed. Users of the Boston Elbow and Utah Arm, in contrast, can control the speed of flexion and extension by contracting their stump muscles more or less intensely. The Utah Arm is a second-generation Boston Elbow and costs about twice as much.

The Boston Elbow is undoubtedly a good arm, but how good are the laws that constitute public policy regarding its use? These laws do not maximize diffusion of the Elbow and, more generally, they discriminate among potential users on the basis of military service, work history, and other particulars. As a result, government may provide one person with a Boston Elbow and a similarly disabled individual with a cable-controlled prosthesis or none at all. Non-prosthetic alternatives to the Boston Elbow are distributed according to the same rules.

That people with the same loss may be entitled to different sets of compensatory options raises serious equity considerations. Amputation is a trauma for all who experience it. The loss of an arm is a loss of functions and meanings, and although compensation can take several forms, none is really adequate. It is possible, however, to mitigate amputation, and some compensatory options suit any one person better than others do. Government could facilitate a match of options and individuals based entirely on medical and other personal characteristics. Many people interviewed for this study expressed disappointment and even outrage that factors other than need seem to be shaping public policy.

Ideally, all disabled people would have the opportunity for maximum compensation. Many do not because government restricts the distribution of technology and other compensatory measures. But these policies are neither irrational nor substantially more inequitable than those that distribute other resources. Rather the Boston Elbow and other compensatory options serve the purposes of larger programs and reflect societal decisions about what is important. Support for the military, for example, translates into generous veterans benefits, and a stable industrial workforce requires a system of compensation for work-related injuries. This is not to say that programmatic goals are unambiguous or that political and economic constraints do not warp programmatic action. It is only to put policy made for the Boston Elbow in context: these laws are neither aberrant nor arbitrary. This study has revealed ironies in the public policy that diffuses the Boston Elbow, but it does not challenge in any fundamental way the match of veteran, worker, and citizen to their respective compensatory arrays. That is another study. Besides, compensatory strategies are necessarily grounded in the meaning of loss, and this includes its meaning for the polity.

References

Abul-Haj, Cary, and Neville Hogan. 1981. "The Design of an Elbow Prosthesis Simulator for Testing Neurophysiologically-Based Controllers."
Unpub. paper, Laboratory for Biomechanics and Human Rehabilitation, M.I.T., Cambridge, Mass.

Allen, Thomas J. 1977. *Managing the Flow of Technology.* Cambridge, Mass.:
M.I.T. Press.

Allen, Thomas J. 1981. "The Role of Person-to-Person Communications in
the Transfer of Technological Knowledge." In Edward B. Roberts,
Robert I. Levy, Stan N. Finkelstein, Jay Moskowitz, and Edward J.
Sondik, eds., *Biomedical Innovation.* Cambridge, Mass.: M.I.T. Press,
pp. 34–49.

American Academy of Orthopaedic Surgeons. 1981. *Atlas of Limb Prosthetics: Surgical and Prosthetic Principles.* St. Louis: C. V. Mosby.

American Association for the Advancement of Science. 1980. "Research
Support from the Veterans Administration." *Bulletins on Science and
Technology for the Handicapped* 1(3): 4–9.

Anderrson, Kjell, and Stig Berg. 1975. "The Relationship Between Some
Psychological Factors and the Outcome of Medical Rehabilitation."
Scandinavian Journal of Rehabilitation Medicine 7: 166–170.

Ayers, William R. 1977. "The Application of Technology to Handicapping
Conditions and for Handicapped Individuals." In *Proceedings of the
White House Conference on Handicapped Individuals,* I: 19–34.

Banta, H. David, and Clyde J. Behney. 1981. "Policy Formulation and
Technology Assessment." *Milbank Memorial Fund Quarterly* 59(3):
445–479.

Berkowitz, Monroe. 1976. "Public Policy Towards Disability: The Numbers, the Programs and Some Economic Problems." In National Research Council, *Science and Technology in the Service of the Physically*

Handicapped, II. Washington, D.C.: National Academy of Sciences, pp. 34–66.

Berkowitz, Monroe. 1981. "Social Policy and the Disabled." Paper presented at Conference on the Implications for Social Security of Research on Invalidity, Vienna, April 1–3.

Better, Sybil R., Phillip R. Fine, Diane Simison, Gordon H. Doss, Richard T. Walls, and Don E. McLaughlin. 1979. "Disability Benefits as Disincentives to Rehabilitation." *Milbank Memorial Fund Quarterly* 57(3): 412–427.

Bizzi, Emilio, Neri Accornero, William Chapple, and Neville Hogan. 1980. "Processes Underlying Arm Trajectory Formation." In *Brain Mechanisms of Perceptual Awareness & Purposeful Behavior.* New York: Raven Press, 1980.

Bliss, James. 1982. Remarks before Capitol Conference on Technology and Handicapped People (principal sponsor, American Association for the Advancement of Science), Washington, D.C., Sept. 29–Oct. 1.

Bonafede, Don. 1982. "Nimmo Admits He Was Sometimes the Last to Know What the VA Was Up To." *National Journal,* Oct. 9: 1715–1718.

Bowe, Frank. 1980. *Rehabilitating America: Toward Independence for Disabled and Elderly People.* New York: Harper and Row.

Brooks, Harvey. 1980. "Technology, Evolution, and Purpose." *Daedalus* 109(1): 65–82.

Brown, Janet Welsh, and Martha Ross Redden. 1979. *A Research Agenda on Science and Technology for the Handicapped.* American Association for the Advancement of Science Report No. 79-R-15. Washington, D.C.: AAAS.

Burkhauser, Richard V., and Robert H. Haveman. 1982. *Disability and Work: The Economics of American Policy.* Baltimore: Johns Hopkins University Press.

Business Week. Sept. 22, 1980. "Technology's New Promise for the Handicapped," 46B–46P.

Canestrari, R., and P. E. Ricci Bitti. 1978. "Psychology of the Hearing-Impaired and Differential Psychological Reactions to Prosthetic Rehabilitation." *Audiology* 17: 32–42.

Cater, Morrow. 1982. "Trimming the Disability Rolls: Changing the Rules During the Game?" *National Journal,* Sept. 4: 1512–1514.

Childress, Dudley S. 1973. "Powered Limb Prostheses: Their Clinical Significance." *IEEE Transactions on Biomedical Engineering* 20(3): 200–207.

Childress, Dudley S. 1981. "Upper Limb Prosthetic Systems: External Power in Upper Limb Prosthetics." In American Academy of Orthopaedic Surgeons, *Atlas of Limb Prosthetics: Surgical and Prosthetic Principles.* St. Louis: C. V. Mosby, pp. 144–159.

Cleland, Max. 1980. *Strong at the Broken Places.* New York: Berkley.

Coleman, J. S., E. Katz, and H. Menzel. 1966. *Medical Innovation: A Diffusion Study.* Indianapolis: Bobbs-Merrill.

Conley, Ronald W. 1965. *The Economics of Vocational Rehabilitation.* Baltimore: Johns Hopkins University Press.

Corcoran, Paul J. 1978. "Rehabilitation: Definitions and Concepts." Paper presented at VA Rehabilitation Medicine Workshop, Roanoke, Va., Sept. 25.

Corcoran, Paul J. 1981. "Rehabilitation in the Medical School Curriculum." Keynote talk, Rehabilitation in the Teaching Center Workshop, Harvard Medical School, Cambridge, Mass., May 9.

Crewe, Nancy M., and Irving Kenneth Zola, eds. 1983. *Independent Living for Physically Disabled People.* Washington, D.C.: Jossey-Bass.

Davies, Elizabeth J., Barbara R. Friz, and Frank W. Clippinger. 1970. "Amputees and Their Prostheses." *Artificial Limbs* 14(2): 19–48.

DeJong, Gerben, and Raymond Lifchez. 1983. "Physical Disability and Public Policy." *Scientific American* 248(6): 40–49.

Disabled American Veterans (DAV). 1983. "Legislative Resolutions, 1982–1983." Notes, Boston.

Dorf, Richard C. 1974. *Technology, Society and Man.* San Francisco: Boyd and Fraser.

Dudek, Richard A., and Charles W. Brewer. 1978. "Human Rehabilitation Techniques: A Technology Assessment." Paper presented at Annual Meeting of the American Association for the Advancement of Science, Feb. 12–17.

Fay, Frederick A. 1982. "Fitting Technology to the Handicapped Human Being." In Virginia Stern and Martha Redden, eds., *Technology for Independent Living.* Washington, D.C.: American Association for the Advancement of Science, pp. 44–45.

Feinsilber, Mike. 1981. "VA Finds Waste at NY Office." *Philadelphia Inquirer,* Dec. 25: 17-A.

Fiske, Edward B. 1982. "Setback for Handicapped." *New York Times,* June 30, II 2:5.

Foulds, Richard A., and Brenda L. Lund. 1976. *Proceedings: 1976 Conference on Systems and Devices for the Disabled.* Boston: Biomedical Engineering Center, Tufts–New England Medical Center.

Friedmann, Lawrence W. 1978. *The Psychological Rehabilitation of the Amputee.* Springfield, Ill.: Chas. C. Thomas.

Fulford, G. E., and M. J. Hall. 1968. *Amputation and Prosthesis: A Survey in North-West Europe and North America.* Bristol, Eng.: John Wright and Sons.

Gaylin, Willard. 1978. "In the Beginning: Helpless and Dependent." In Willard Gaylin, Ira Glasser, Steven Marcus, and David J. Rothman, *Doing Good: The Limits of Benevolence.* New York: Pantheon, pp. 1–38.

Gaylin, Willard, Ira Glasser, Steven Marcus, and David J. Rothman. 1978. *Doing Good: The Limits of Benevolence.* New York: Pantheon.

Goldin, George J., Sally L. Perry, Reuben J. Margolin, and Bernard A. Stotsky. 1972. *Dependency and Its Implications for Rehabilitation.* Lexington, Mass.: D. C. Heath.

Gordon, Gerald, Ann E. MacEachron, and G. Lawrence Fisher. 1982. "A Contingency Model for the Design of Problem-Solving Research Programs: A Perspective on Diffusion Research." In John B. McKinlay, ed., *Technology and the Future of Health Care.* Boston: M.I.T. Press, pp. 197–228.

Greenberg, Barbara, and Robert A. Derzon. 1981. "Determining Health Insurance Coverage of Technology: Problems and Options." *Medical Care* 19(10): 967–978.

Greenhouse, Linda. 1982. "Schools Backed on Limiting Aid to Handicapped." *New York Times,* June 29, II 4:1.

Gusfield, Joseph. 1981. *The Culture of Public Problems: Drinking-Driving and the Symbolic Order.* Chicago: University of Chicago Press.

Haberer, Joseph, ed. 1973. *Technology and the Future of Man.* South Bend, Ind.: Purdue University Press.

Health Insurance Association of America (HIAA). 1979. *Compensation Systems Available to Disabled Persons in the United States.* Washington, D.C.: Health Insurance Institute.

Herberts, P., L. Korner, K. Caine, and L. Wensby. 1980. "Rehabilitation of Unilateral Below-Elbow Amputees with Myoelectric Prostheses." *Scandinavian Journal of Rehabilitation Medicine* 12: 123–128.

Hetherington, Robert W., Carl E. Hopkins, and Martin I. Roemer. 1975. *Health Insurance Plans: Promise and Performance.* New York: John Wiley and Sons.

Howards, Irving, Henry P. Brehm, and Saad Z. Nagi. 1980. *Disability: From Social Problem to Federal Program.* New York: Praeger.

Jacobsen, Stephen C., David F. Knutti, Richard T. Johnson, and Harold H. Sears. 1982. "Development of the Utah Artificial Arm." *IEEE Transactions on Biomedical Engineering* BME-29(4): 249–269.

Jerard, Robert B. 1970. "Design of a Multiple Degree of Freedom Prosthesis." Unpub. master's thesis, M.I.T. Department of Mechanical Engineering, Cambridge, Mass.

Jerard, Robert B., T. Walley Williams, III, and Cord W. Ohlenbusch. 1974. "Practical Design of an EMG Controlled Above-Elbow Prosthesis." *Proceedings of the 1974 Conference on Engineering Devices for Rehabilitation.* Boston: Tufts Biomedical Engineering Center, pp. 73–77.

Kaplan, Deborah. 1982. "The Consumer and Basic Engineering Research: Problems in Coinvention." In Virginia Stern and Martha Redden, eds., *Technology for Independent Living.* Washington, D.C.: American Association for the Advancement of Science, pp. 91–92.

Kenedi, R. M. 1969. "In Search of the Ideal Limb Concept." In George Murdoch, ed., *Prosthetic and Orthotic Practice*. London: Edward Arnold, pp. 37–40.

Kennedy, Lenna. 1982. "SSI: Trends and Changes, 1974–80." *Social Security Bulletin* 45(7): 3–12.

Kerstein, Morris D. 1980. "Surgeons Neglect Plight of Leg Amputees." *Medical World News*, Oct. 27: 71.

Kidder, Tracy. 1981. *The Soul of a New Machine*. Boston: Little, Brown.

Klein, Robert. 1981. *Wounded Men, Broken Promises*. New York: Macmillan.

Kornbluh, Marvin. 1981. *Technology to Aid Disabled Persons: Views from the Handicapped Community*. Prepared at the request of the House Committee on Science and Technology, Subcommittee on Science, Research, and Technology. Washington, D.C.: Congressional Research Service.

Korner, Lars. 1979. "Sensory Feedback for Motorized Hand Prostheses." *International Journal of Rehabilitation Research* 2(3): 386–387.

Lando, Mordechai E., Alice V. Farley, and Mary A. Brown. 1982. "Recent Trends in the Social Security Disability Insurance Program." *Social Security Bulletin* 45(8): 3–14.

LaRocca, Joseph, and Jerry S. Turem. 1978. *The Application of Technological Developments to Physically Disabled People*. Washington, D.C.: Urban Institute.

LeBlanc, Maurice A. 1971. "Clinical Evaluation of Externally Powered Prosthetic Elbows." *Artificial Limbs* 19(1): 70–77.

Levitan, Sar A., and Karen A. Cleary. 1973. *Old Wars Remain Unfinished*. Baltimore: Johns Hopkins University Press.

Levitan, Sar A., and Robert Taggart. 1977. *Jobs for the Disabled*. Baltimore: Johns Hopkins University Press.

Liberty Mutual Insurance Company. 1984. *Annual Report 1983*. Boston: Liberty Mutual.

Madjid, Hadi. 1982. "Everything Transitory Is Symbolic." In Virginia Stern and Martha Redden, eds., *Technology for Independent Living*. Washington, D.C.: American Association for the Advancement of Science, pp. 97–101.

Mann, Robert W. 1973. "Tradeoffs at the Man-Machine Interface in Cybernetic Prostheses/Orthoses." In R. M. Kenedi, ed., *Perspectives in Biomedical Engineering*. London: Macmillan, pp. 73–77.

Mann, Robert W. 1981. "Cybernetic Limb Prosthesis: The Distinguished ALZA Lecture." *Annals of Biomedical Engineering* 9: 1–43.

Mann, Robert W., and Stephen D. Reimers. 1970. "Kinesthetic Sensing for the EMG Controlled 'Boston Elbow.'" *IEEE Transactions on Man-Machine Systems* MMS-11(1): 110–115.

Marris, Peter. 1974. *Loss and Change*. Garden City, N.Y.: Anchor, Doubleday.

162

References

Massachusetts Division of Industrial Accidents. 1982. "Workmen's Compensation." Fact sheet, Boston.

Massachusetts Medical Assistance Program (Medicaid), Department of Public Welfare. 1981. "Durable Medical Equipment Manual." Boston.

Massachusetts Rehabilitation Commission (MRC). 1982. *Annual Report for Fiscal Year 1981.* Boston: MRC.

Massachusetts Rehabilitation Commission (MRC). 1983. *Annual Report for Fiscal Year 1982.* Boston: MRC.

McKenzie, D. S. 1969. "Functional Replacement of the Upper Extremity Today." In George Murdoch, ed., *Prosthetic and Orthotic Practice.* London: Edward Arnold, pp. 363–376.

McLaurin, Colin. 1982. Remarks before Capitol Conference on Technology and Handicapped People (principal sponsor, American Association for the Advancement of Science), Washington, D.C., Sept. 29–Oct. 1.

McManus, L. A. 1981. "Evaluation of Disability Insurance Savings Due to Beneficiary Rehabilitation." *Social Security Bulletin* 44(2): 19.

Meislin, Richard J. 1981. "Outlays of Millions Required to Meet U.S. Standards." *New York Times,* Jan. 28, II 1:4.

Melvin, John L., and Saad Z. Nagi. 1970. "Factors in Behavioral Responses to Impairments." *Archives of Physical Medicine and Rehabilitation* (Sept.): 552–557.

Mittelmann, Michael, and Jan Settele. 1982. "Insurance Reimbursement Mechanisms for Rehabilitation Equipment and Environmental Modifications." *Archives of Physical Medicine and Rehabilitation* 63(June): 279–283.

Moskowitz, Jay, Stan N. Finkelstein, Robert I. Levy, Edward B. Roberts, and Edward J. Sondik. 1981. "Biomedical Innovation: The Challenge and the Process." In Edward B. Roberts, Robert I. Levy, Stan N. Finkelstein, Jay Moskowitz, and Edward J. Sondik, eds., *Biomedical Innovation.* Cambridge, Mass.: M.I.T. Press, pp. 1–17.

Murdoch, George. 1969. "An Introduction to Clinical Prescription and Practice." In George Murdoch, ed., *Prosthetic and Orthotic Practice.* London: Edward Arnold, pp. 1–6.

Murdoch, George, ed. 1969. *Prosthetic and Orthotic Practice.* London: Edward Arnold.

Murdoch, George, and John Hughes. 1973. "Clinical and Biomedical Aspects of Current Prosthetic Practice." In R. M. Kenedi, ed., *Perspectives in Biomedical Engineering.* London: Macmillan, pp. 67–72.

Muthard, J. E. 1980. *Putting Rehabilitation Knowledge to Use.* Gainesville: University of Florida Rehabilitation Research Institute.

Nagi, Saad Z. 1969. *Disability and Rehabilitation: Legal, Clinical and Self-Concepts and Measurements.* Columbus: Ohio State University Press.

Nagi, Saad Z. 1976. "An Epidemiology of Disability Among Adults in the United States." *Milbank Memorial Fund Quarterly* 56(4): 439–467.

National Center for Health Statistics (NCHS), U.S. Department of Health and Human Services. 1980. National Health Interview Survey 1977, Series 10, No. 135, DHHS (PHS)81-1563. Washington, D.C. In Theta Technology Corp., *Prosthetic Limbs Market.* Wethersfield, Conn.: Theta Technology, p. 11.

National Institute of Handicapped Research (NIHR), U.S. Department of Education. 1981. *Long-Range Plan.* Washington, D.C.: NIHR.

National Research Council (NRC). 1976. *Science and Technology in the Service of the Physically Handicapped,* I, II, and Summary. Washington, D.C.: National Academy of Sciences.

New York Times. May 1, 1982. 14:3.

New York Times. Nov. 12, 1982. 23:1.

New York Times. April 26, 1983. II 20:1.

Noble, John H., Jr. 1976. "The Limits of Cost-Benefit Analysis as a Guide to Priority-Setting in Rehabilitation." In National Research Council, *Science and Technology in the Service of the Physically Handicapped,* II. Washington, D.C.: National Academy of Sciences, pp. 1–33.

Obermann, C. Esco. 1965. *A History of Vocational Rehabilitation in America.* Minneapolis: T. C. Denison.

Office of Technology Assessment (OTA). 1982. *Technology and Handicapped People,* OTA-H-179. Washington, D.C.: U.S. Government Printing Office.

O'Sullivan, Susan B., Karen E. Cullen, and Thomas J. Schmitz. 1981. *Physical Rehabilitation: Evaluation and Treatment Procedures.* Philadelphia: F. A. Davis.

Peizer, Edward. 1981. "Research Trends in Upper Limb Prosthetics." In American Academy of Orthopaedic Surgeons, *Atlas of Limb Prosthetics: Surgical and Prosthetic Principles.* St. Louis: C. V. Mosby, pp. 219–258.

Peizer, Edward, Donald W. Wright, and Thomas Pirrello, Jr. 1970. "Perspectives on the Use of External Power in Upper-Extremity Prostheses." *Bulletin of Prosthetics Research,* BPR 10-13: 25–38.

Pfrommer, Margaret. 1982. Testimony before Senate Committee on Labor and Human Resources and Subcommittee on Science, Research, and Technology of the House Committee on Science and Technology, Washington, D.C., Sept. 29.

Philipson, Lennart, Dudley S. Childress, and John Strysik. 1981. "Digital Approaches to Myoelectric State Control of Prostheses." *Bulletin of Prosthetics Research,* BPR 10-36: 3–11.

Pirsig, Robert M. 1974. *Zen and the Art of Motorcycle Maintenance.* New York: Bantam.

Piven, Frances Fox, and Richard A. Cloward. 1977. *Poor People's Movements.* New York: Random House.

Post, James E. 1976. *Risk and Response.* Lexington, Mass.: D. C. Heath.

Price, Daniel N. 1980. "Workers' Compensation: 1978 Program Update." *Social Security Bulletin* 43(10): 3–10.

Rabinowitz, Herbert S., and Spiro B. Mitsos. 1964. "Rehabilitation as

Planned Social Change: A Conceptual Framework." *Journal of Health and Human Behavior* 1(1): 2–14.

Rashkow, Ilona N. 1978. *The Veterans Pension Program Past, Present, and Future.* Hearings before Subcommittee on Compensation, Pension, and Insurance of the House Committee on Veterans Affairs. Washington, D.C.: U.S. Government Printing Office.

Rehab Group, Inc. 1979. *Digest of Data of Persons with Disabilities.* Washington, D.C.: Department of Health, Education, and Welfare.

Rehabilitation Services Administration (RSA), U.S. Department of Education. 1982. *Annual Report Fiscal Year 1981.* Washington, D.C.: RSA.

Reiser, Stanley Joel. 1978. *Medicine and the Reign of Technology.* New York: Cambridge University Press.

Rettig, Richard. 1978. "Lessons Learned from the End-Stage Renal Disease Experience." In Richard H. Egdahl and Paul M. Gertman, eds., *Technology and the Quality of Health Care.* Germantown, Md.: Aspen Systems Corp., pp. 153–174.

Rettig, Richard. 1980. "The Federal Government and Medical Technology: Crossing Policy and Management Thresholds." *Policy Sciences.* 11: 343–356.

Roberts, Edward B. 1981. "Influences on Innovation: Extrapolations to Biomedical Technology." In Edward B. Roberts, Robert I. Levy, Stan N. Finkelstein, Jay Moskowitz, and Edward J. Sondik, eds., *Biomedical Innovation.* Cambridge, Mass.: M.I.T. Press.

Roberts, Edward B., Robert I. Levy, Stan N. Finkelstein, Jay Moskowitz, and Edward J. Sondik, eds. 1981. *Biomedical Innovation.* Cambridge, Mass.: M.I.T. Press.

Rogers, Everett M. 1981. "Diffusion of Innovations: An Overview." In Edward B. Roberts, Robert I. Levy, Stan N. Finkelstein, Jay Moskowitz, and Edward J. Sondik, eds., *Biomedical Innovation.* Cambridge, Mass.: M.I.T. Press, pp. 75–97.

Rothchild, Ronald. 1965. *Design of an Externally Powered Artificial Elbow for Electromyographic Control.* Unpub. master's thesis, M.I.T. Department of Mechanical Engineering, Cambridge, Mass.

Russell, Louise B. 1977. "The Diffusion of Hospital Technologies: Some Econometric Evidence." *Journal of Human Resources* 7: 482–502.

Schon, Donald A. 1967. *Technology and Change.* New York: Delacorte.

Schon, Donald. 1970. "The Blindness System." *Public Interest,* no. 18: 25–37.

Sclove, Richard E. 1982. "Decision-Making in a Democracy." *Bulletin of the Atomic Scientists* (May): 44–49.

Scott, Robert A. 1969. *The Making of Blind Men.* New York: Russell Sage.

Shriver, Donald W., Jr. 1973. "Invisible Doorway: Hope as a Technological Virtue." In Joseph Haberer, ed., *Technology and the Future of Man.* South Bend, Ind.: Purdue University Press, pp. 7–17.

Smith, Richard T., and Abraham M. Lilienfield. 1972. *The Social Security Disability Program: An Evaluation Study*. Washington, D.C.: Department of Health, Education, and Welfare.

Soyer, David. 1963. "The Right to Fail." *Social Work* 8(July): 72–78.

Steiner, Gilbert Y. 1971. *The State of Welfare*. Washington, D.C.: Brookings Institution.

Stern, Virginia, and Martha Redden, eds. 1982. *Technology for Independent Living*. Washington, D.C.: American Association for the Advancement of Science.

Stevens, Robert, and Rosemary Stevens. 1974. *Welfare Medicine in America*. New York: Free Press.

Stewart, Robert E., and William M. Bernstock. 1977. *Veterans Administration Prosthetic and Sensory Aids Program since World War II*. Washington, D.C.: Veterans Administration.

Stone, Deborah A. 1979. "Diagnosis and the Dole: The Function of Illness in American Distributive Politics." *Journal of Health Politics, Policy and Law* 4(3): 507–521.

Stone, Deborah A. 1984. *The Disabled State*. Philadelphia: Temple University Press.

Sussman, Marvin B. 1965. "Occupational Sociology and Rehabilitation." In Marvin B. Sussman, ed., *Sociology and Rehabilitation*. Washington, D.C.: American Sociological Association.

Sussman, Marvin B., ed. 1965. *Sociology and Rehabilitation*. Washington, D.C.: American Sociological Association.

Swaine, Michael. 1983. "Giving the Disabled an Extension of the Will to Dance." *Infoworld* 5(13): 23–24.

Tanenbaum, Sandra J. 1984. *The Boston Elbow*. Office of Technology Assessment, Health Technology Case Study No. 29 for *Federal Policies and the Medical Devices Industry*. Washington, D.C.: U.S. Government Printing Office.

Theta Technology Corp. 1981. *Prosthetic Limbs Market*. Report No. 150. Wethersfield, Conn.: Theta Technology.

Thompson, Frank J. 1981. *Health Policy and Bureaucracy: Politics and Implementation*. Cambridge, Mass.: M.I.T. Press.

Tobias, James. 1982. "Grassroots Rehabilitation Technology and the Delivery System: Getting Things Done at Independent Living Centers and Models in the Nonsystem." In Virginia Stern and Martha Redden, eds., *Technology for Independent Living*. Washington, D.C.: American Association for the Advancement of Science, pp. 102–107.

U.S. Congress. 1977. House Committee on Science and Technology, *Report of the Panel on Research Programs to Aid the Handicapped*, 95th Cong., 1st sess. Washington, D.C.: U.S. Government Printing Office.

U.S. Congress. 1978. House Committee on Science and Technology, *Report of the Panel on Research Programs to Aid the Handicapped*, 95th Congress, 2nd sess. Washington, D.C.: U.S. Government Printing Office.

Utterback, James M. 1974. "Innovation in Industry and the Diffusion of Technology." *Science* 183: 620–626.

Varela, Rita A. 1983. "Changing Social Attitudes and Legislation Regarding Disability." In Nancy M. Crewe and Irving Kenneth Zola, eds., *Independent Living for Physically Disabled People*. Washington, D.C.: Jossey-Bass, pp. 28–48.

Verville, Richard E. 1979. "The Disabled, Rehabilitation, and Current Public Policy." *Journal of Rehabilitation* (April/May/June): 48–51, 89.

Veterans Administration (VA). 1981. "Service-Connected Disability Compensation Information: Persons on the Rolls as of the End of December 1980." Controlled Report No. 1B 04-81-5.

Veterans Administration (VA). 1982a. "Disability Compensation: Basic Rates." 38 U.S.C. 314, Oct. Washington, D.C.: U.S. Government Printing Office.

Veterans Administration (VA). 1982b. *Federal Benefits for Veterans and Dependents*. IS-1 fact sheet, Jan. 1. Washington, D.C.: U.S. Government Printing Office.

Veterans Administration Prosthetic and Sensory Aids Service. 1983. "Prosthetic and Sensory Aids Service Briefing for Professional Services." Unpub. material. Washington, D.C.

Weizenbaum, Joseph. 1979. *Computer Power and Human Reason*. San Francisco: W. H. Freeman.

Wessen, Albert. 1965. "The Apparatus of Rehabilitation: An Organizational Analysis." In Marvin B. Sussman, ed., *Sociology and Rehabilitation*. Washington, D.C.: American Sociological Association.

Whipple, Lee. 1980. *Whole Again*. Ossining, N.Y.: Caroline House.

Wiener, Norbert. 1951. "Problems of Sensory Prosthesis." *Bulletin of the American Mathematical Society* 56(1): 27–35.

Will, George F. 1983. "A Magna Carta for the Handicapped." Reprinted in *Summerfest* 4: 8.

Williams, T. Walley, III. 1976. "Clinical Application of the Improved Boston Arm." In Richard A. Foulds and Brenda L. Lund, eds., *Proceedings: 1976 Conference on Systems and Devices for the Disabled*. Boston: Biomedical Engineering Center, Tufts–New England Medical Center, pp. 109–113.

Wilson, A. Bennett, Jr. 1969. "Some Observations on Upper-Extremity Prosthetics." In George Murdoch, ed., *Prosthetic and Orthotic Practice*. London: Edward Arnold, pp. 331–335.

Wilson, A. Bennett, Jr. 1981. "History of amputation surgery and prosthetics." In American Academy of Orthopaedic Surgeons, *Atlas of Limb Prosthetics: Surgical and Prosthetic Principles*. St. Louis: C. V. Mosby, pp. 3–13.

Winner, Langdon. 1977. *Autonomous Technology: Technics-Out-of-Control as a Theme in Political Thought*. Cambridge, Mass.: M.I.T. Press.

Winner, Langdon. 1980. "Do Artifacts Have Politics?" *Daedalus* 109(1): 121–136.

Zafra, Victor. 1980. "BMD Update." *Medical Devices, Diagnostics, and Instrumentation Reports: The Grey Sheet,* Oct., pp. 8–9.

Zola, Irving Kenneth. 1980. "Involving the Consumer in the Rehabilitation Process: Easier Said Than Done." Paper presented at Tufts University Conference on Technology for the Handicapped, Boston, Mass., Sept. 7.

Zola, Irving Kenneth. 1982. *Missing Pieces: A Chronicle of Living With a Disability.* Philadelphia: Temple University Press.

Index